# R3R1 | THE SALES FORMULA FOR SUCCESS

**RUSSELL M. RUSH**

Copyright © 2017 Russell M. Rush.

All rights reserved. No part of this book may be reproduced, stored, or transmitted by any means—whether auditory, graphic, mechanical, or electronic—without written permission of the author, except in the case of brief excerpts used in critical articles and reviews. Unauthorized reproduction of any part of this work is illegal and is punishable by law.

ISBN: 978-1-4834-6557-9 (sc)
ISBN: 978-1-4834-6559-3 (hc)
ISBN: 978-1-4834-6558-6 (e)

Library of Congress Control Number: 2017902319

Because of the dynamic nature of the Internet, any web addresses or links contained in this book may have changed since publication and may no longer be valid. The views expressed in this work are solely those of the author and do not necessarily reflect the views of the publisher, and the publisher hereby disclaims any responsibility for them.

Any people depicted in stock imagery provided by Thinkstock are models, and such images are being used for illustrative purposes only. Certain stock imagery © Thinkstock.

Lulu Publishing Services rev. date: 4/12/2017

# CONTENTS

Dedication .................................................................................. ix
Introduction ................................................................................ xi
The Early Years ............................................................................ 1
The Beginning .............................................................................. 7
The Discovery Timeline ............................................................... 11
    The First Big Idea
    The Second Big Idea
    The Experiment
    The Formula
R3R1—The Sales Formula for Success ........................................ 21
Relate ......................................................................................... 31
    First Impressions
    The Warm-Up
    Qualifying Prospects
    Answering Questions
    The Why
    Insurmountable Obstacles
Reason ....................................................................................... 51
    Foundation of Reasoning
    Company Presentation
    Differentiation Statements
    Mission Statement
    Outcomes
    Speed Messaging
    The Expert
    The Unconscious Mind

    Yes, Maybe, No
    The Smokescreen
    Liars
    Suitability
    Commitment Questions
    Why Logic

Resolve ............................................................................97
    Money
        Duration
        Price/Cost Analysis
    Needs
    The Product
    Selection
    Incentives
        Moral Suasion, Reasoning, and Education
    The Close
        Time to Decide
        Gifting, Reassurance, and Cancellations

R3R1 Sales Process..........................................................127
    Using All Three Rs

Results ............................................................................137

The R3R1 Recap.............................................................141

Insights ...........................................................................145
    The Post-Mortem
    Bought or Sold
    Demand
    Keeping Score
    Execution
    Strike While the Iron is Hot!
    Changing Lose to Win
    Playing the Right Card
    Conviction

Focus
Stick to Your Knitting
The Need for Practice
Self-Discipline
Perfection!

Conclusion ................................................................................. 179
About the Author ..................................................................... 181

# DEDICATION

Kathleen was born in Niagara Falls, New York, but relocated to Wichita, Kansas, in the early 1970s for her father's work. We met in 1981 and married in 1982, and she has been my wife and partner ever since. Kathleen has worked with me directly on every major business project since 1982 and was instrumental in the development of our first and second software programs. She co-developed many of the concepts, but she outright developed many of them on her own. Anyone who has worked with us over the many years knows how instrumental she has been in the development of the products and services that we brought to market. This book is a culmination of our collaboration over more than thirty years, and I wish to dedicate this endeavor to her constant support.

# INTRODUCTION

Over the years, through many highs and lows, I've had the good fortune to work on quite a few exciting things in a wide array of industries and roles. One of my most challenging but most fulfilling roles has been in sales and business development. Starting at a very young age, I've been fascinated by sales—the psychology of it, the challenge of it, the punch in the stomach of failure, and the incredible joy of success. As one can imagine, throughout the years I've developed quite a history of successes and some failures, but in the end, I've been able to develop what I feel is a unique approach to sales. With this book, *R3R1: The Sales Formula for Success*, I hope to share with you a method, a style, an approach, a *formula* that you can put into practice today that will lead to results, just as it has with me throughout my career.

Of course, right now you might be asking, "Yeah, well, a lot of people have a sales method. Why should I listen to what you have to say?" Know what? You'd be right to ask that question! Every prospect of yours is asking the same thing about you, so why shouldn't you ask the same of this book? If you're asking that question, then you're already leaps and bounds above other salespeople because asking the right questions is *so* important!

So before we jump into the meat of the R3R1 formula, I'd like to tell you a little bit about myself and my history to set the stage for what you are about to learn. You'll begin to understand a bit more about me, and perhaps you'll be able to relate my experience to your current situation. You see, one of the joys of climbing the ladder in sales is that someday you'll be able to impart your knowledge to someone else. I took great pride in watching salespeople who followed my direction, guidance, mentorship, and advice become successes themselves. When one creates a book to share this information, that's the implicit goal: to share knowledge and experiences and help others succeed. That's what this book is intended to do.

# THE EARLY YEARS

Now, what sales formula introduction wouldn't be complete without a story about a pig? That's right, a story about a pig. Why? Simple ... everyone that's in the sales universe starts somewhere, and everyone has a story that can turn back the clock to remind them that *this* event had more of an impact on their life than they thought. As I was developing this book and thinking of the many life events that brought me to where I am today, I decided I needed to start with the pig story. So pay attention—believe it or not, this comes back later on!

I spent my early years living on a farm close to the small town of Maize, Kansas. We grew watermelons on our farm, and as kids, my brothers and I would sell a portion of the crop from our driveway to passersby. We would fashion a high-tech advertising campaign consisting of a black sign with white letters that said "WATERMELONS." We would fill an old bathtub with ice to keep our watermelons nice and cool and wait for potential customers to pull up.

"How much for your watermelons, son?"

"Three cents a pound, sir."

"Okay ... I'll take one."

We were off to the races. I would take a watermelon out of the old bathtub where it was submerged in icy water and say, "What do think about this one?" The prospect would routinely *thump* the watermelon to determine if it produced the right sound for a perfectly ripe melon and then say "That looks good." We would weigh the watermelon on an old bathroom scale and let them know the cost of their selection—sixty cents. The prospect would pay us and drive away, but now they were our customer. *Success!* That was *our* sixty cents. The money earned from our venture was divided evenly.

In addition to growing watermelons, we raised a breed of pigs on the farm called Durocs. Durocs are unusual because they are red in color and not as aggressive as other breeds of pigs. We had several sows and one boar, and they were bred in what would now be considered a free-range environment.

My father was what one would call a gentleman farmer. He understood the nature of farming—the costs, time, and effort associated with the entire process, just as any businessperson would know their costs, time, and effort related to finding a new client and maintaining that relationship. In the grand scheme, what he did is no different from any business owner or salesperson. There is a cost to everything!

When the pigs that were known as feeder pigs got to a certain age, my father would load them in a trailer that he would tow behind our big old pickup truck and head into town to sell them at the stockyards. Each time, he would take just one of us young boys with him, which was a big deal, because after the check from the sale was deposited, the brother that helped received his reward—a giant glazed donut or two from the local donut shop.

Remember, this is rural Kansas, so this is a pretty big deal in the life of a farm kid!

Then came the day when I was chosen to be the helper. So, as usual, we loaded up the pigs—around twenty of them—and headed for town. Everything was going well—it was a pleasant ride, lovely scenery. But then my father started to get a little ... fidgety. He was looking in the mirror and looking pretty serious while he began muttering some indistinct sounds. Something was going on that was a *lot* more interesting than just staring out the window, so I checked in the large sideview mirror only to notice that one of our pigs was making a break for it ... as we were traveling along at fifty-five miles per hour down the highway!

Perhaps that pig knew what was in store for him (they are very perceptive animals, you know) and decided that this was his chance. After climbing on the backs of the others, he headed toward the back of the trailer—and off he went! Needless to say, my father wasn't very happy with all of this, and as I watched this pig flip and tumble down the highway, my dad slowed the truck down to pull over and assess the damage.

Running back to find out what remained of the pig, we came to see that he miraculously got up on all fours, got his wits about him, and then made a break for the nearest hedgerow of trees until he was out of sight. Well, it appeared that this pig's gamble paid off; we certainly couldn't leave nineteen other pigs on a highway to chase one down.

The real problem was that I started to realize that this was the funniest thing I've ever seen in my young life, and the laughter started and wouldn't stop. I simply could not stop laughing! Unfortunately, my father didn't see the humor, as it was his *money* that was bounding away into the trees, so I heard a calm but direct "Shut up" every time the laughter started. He saw one-twentieth of his profits lost. The sad part was, he was in no mood for the celebratory donut. *Failure!* To this day, I blame that squarely on the pig.

So why exactly is this story so important? It was a simple but useful lesson that, in time, would help me understand a lot of things.

# THE BEGINNING

Now, let's move forward—past the pig adventure—to when my official sales career started, right around age seventeen. My brother, Rick, is ten years older than me and was a salesman at a small company in Wichita, Kansas, that manufactured replacement windows and vinyl siding. I asked if I could work for them, and I was given the job as the appointment setter, which was an early version of a telemarketer. I had a list to call, and when a person answered I would rattle off a quick pitch with the goal to set up a face-to-face meeting for the sales team. I had some success! Soon, my brother and his partner, Dennis, agreed to take me along on a few sales calls. I asked if I should wear a tie and was advised to dress more casually.

Dennis had a beard and wore glasses. He was also short, fat, and balding. Dennis walked with a limp from a bout of polio as a child. When we made sales calls, he wore an installer's uniform with his name on a patch on the pocket. I don't know whose idea that was, but it was ingenious. He traded his fancy Tin Man suit for an installer's uniform to disarm the potential customer. There was no way that they would ever detect the high-powered salesperson that Dennis was. When I went with Dennis, I saw my first real salesman in action.

Later, my brother was kind enough to record his presentation so I could listen and learn it. The presentation had many sections and was somewhat complicated, so I would listen to the recording and memorize each step, word for word. I went on my first sales appointment by myself, but I knew early in the call that I'd blown my chance for a sale. I didn't give up, though! Next, I called an older woman (at least, that was my perception at the time; she was probably only forty or so). To my amazement, after hearing my presentation, she agreed to buy siding for her house! My first commission check was massive—well, for a young kid making his first sale.

That was the beginning of my sales, marketing, and management career, and I've never looked back. What I have sold has changed from watermelons to windows, siding, vacuum cleaners, cars, insurance, securities, software, sporting goods, and even senior housing, but I've always continued learning, and I've always continued selling.

I have attended every possible sales training class or seminar and have read hundreds of sales and management books. Early on, I was convinced that being a salesperson was an honorable profession (due in large part to some additional massive commission checks), but more importantly I came to understand that there was a science to selling. Therefore, I dedicated myself to learning the art behind selling: the concepts, strategies, psychology, presentations, formulas, and theories. From what I discovered, I began to create a variety of better sales strategies, better presentations, and better methods to increase my sales and ultimately those commission checks. Eventually, my personal experience and some good old-fashioned trial and error led to the creation of the R3R1 formula that I am sharing with you today.

# THE DISCOVERY TIMELINE

**B**ut what exactly were some of these personal experiences and other opportunities that came up? How did I go from a window-and-siding rookie to an experienced and dedicated sales professional who has developed a reliable method of sales and business development with the R3R1 formula? We'll begin with a bit of a sad story—one I hesitate to share but one that influenced how I began to develop my expertise and my background.

It began when I was about twenty-six years old, working as an agent for The New York Life Insurance Company in Wichita, Kansas. Just as I was growing my insurance agency and formulating an idea that would eventually affect tens of thousands of insurance agents in a *very* positive way, my beautiful twenty-three-month-old daughter, Jourdan, inexplicably suffered a cardiac arrest with no warning at all. Unfortunately, due to extreme anoxia, Jourdan suffered from permanent blindness, mental disability, and quadriplegia. Although our daughter survived almost seventeen years to the day from when she suffered that horrible cardiac arrest, on June 23, 2006, she passed away. Kathleen and I lovingly cared for her at home for the entire seventeen years. This life-altering event put my life, and my career, on a path that I wouldn't probably have otherwise traveled.

## *The First Big Idea*

One day, someone explained to me that a wealthy person could give $10,000 a year to a child or other family member to transfer it out of their estate. I then learned that if they did not take advantage of this yearly gift opportunity, they lost it. The gift could be a source of premiums for a whole life policy inside of an irrevocable trust. If a married couple had two children and sufficient assets, they could gift $40,000 on an annual basis to a trust for the children and use the money to fund an insurance policy.

I presented this concept to my prospects with significant net worth, but I just wasn't reaching them with this idea. Somehow I had to get this point across, because I knew how great this opportunity could be. So, instead of a polished, professional presentation, I created a cartoon. My little animation presentation showed five cows in one corral in the first picture, while also showing one cow being able to move to another corral. I explained to a couple that if all their cows remained in the same corral until they died, they would pay estate taxes on all the cows. However, if the couple would move one cow (the $10,000 gift) out at a time (the annual opportunity) into their kid's corral, they would not be obligated to pay tax on the gifted amount. The corral illustrations began to work, but one question kept coming up—"What if I need the money back during my retirement for my personal use, and I have already gifted it to the kids?"

I searched for some kind of financial analysis program that would demonstrate to the prospect the affordability of making these gifts to their children while at the same time minimizing the unlikely scenario of needing the money back. Keep in mind that this was 1990, and the only financial analysis that was available was a software program that would take the value of the parents' assets and inflate them using an arbitrary inflation rate. I questioned this presentation and asked, "Is this real?" The answer was "No." I asked myself "What is missing from this presentation?" Obviously, a key element would be how much money the parents would spend during retirement, and *that* was the beginning of the formula.

Logically, the person retiring would need more money over time due to inflation. What assets did they own? Stocks? Bonds? Real estate? Did they have a 401(k) plan or defined benefit pension and Social Security? When were they going to retire? What was their life expectancy? Finally, what effect would the annual gifting have on their assets? After realizing what was needed to prepare a comprehensive analysis of a realistic scenario, I searched for a software company that had such a program because I knew that I needed it for my insurance practice. I soon discovered that such a program didn't exist yet. I approached one of the leading financial services software companies, and shortly after that they developed the system based on my formula … *shortly* being four years later, in 1994. I worked closely with the company through multiple versions of the software, and to this day the system is used by thousands of insurance agents. The formula was copied by several other companies.

## *The Second Big Idea*

Since my insurance agency was primarily high–net worth clients, I became very interested in charitable giving and began to analyze how charities, typically large universities, reported to their donors. Specifically, I was focused on charitable giving as it related to a donor-advised fund, which is like a private foundation established within a larger charity. I was also interested in how the assets that were contributed to the donor-advised fund were managed at the various charities. I discovered that financial advisors wanted to manage the assets that were being held by the charities and that the donors wanted more accountability as to where the money would be directed out of the fund (what was done with the granted money). My efforts led me to the development of an online platform for charities and financial companies that provided a solution for charities, financial advisors, and donors. The charity could host the donor-advised fund program; the financial advisor could manage his client's assets that were contributed to the fund; and the donor had a personal dashboard to review funding opportunities as well as financial statements as they related to his charitable gift. Currently, this platform is providing solutions to large charities across the United States.

When Jourdan finally died, I was lost. I decided I needed a much-needed break after twenty-three years in the financial services industry, launching software programs, and caring for a sick child. My wife and I were completely spent, both mentally and physically. Even though I had a two-year non-compete agreement, at the time I was resigned to the fact that I probably had had my last great idea. I had no desire at all to embark on another stressful venture, to be an industry innovator, or to start another company … so the non-compete wasn't an issue in my mind.

# *The Experiment*

But, as with all things, time eventually passes, and opinions once held begin to change. I decided that I needed to go back to work and to start being productive again. I did some consulting for a sporting goods company, analyzing their value chain and evaluating their marketing and pricing. Even though I had worked mainly in the financial services industry, during my early years I sold consumer products, and the idea of the sale of a physical product to an individual customer once again intrigued me.

However, after the consulting project was over, I began to have serious conversations with a large financial company about joining their team to manage a section of their business. The more I thought about it, I realized that I was not ready to return to financial services. So Kathleen and I started discussing our options, and that's when I proposed an experiment.

What if I went into an entirely unrelated business? Could I create a solution for a whole new industry, not knowing anything about it? I was very confident that with my work ethic and my entrepreneurial background, I could pretty much tackle any industry and make an impact.

I found an opportunity in senior housing, which was about as far away from the financial services sector and related software services as I could be. I told Kathleen that this would be an experiment to see if what I believed was true. Could I be dropped into any industry and develop innovation? I believed I would have enough information to understand the entire realm of the business within three to six months, so I went to work!

At first, I was just happy doing a very basic job and not thinking about changing anything, but that quickly changed. I soon discovered that the marketing and sales processes left room for improvement. So I did what I always have done—I started to analyze the sales process and began to ask questions. Were the flaws I was discovering limited to this company, or did they impact the entire industry? I studied every aspect of the industry and proceeded to develop a sales process. At this point in my so-called experiment, I was working as a salesperson for a senior housing company. Utilizing the sales process that I developed for myself, I could fill a brand-new community significantly faster than the average salesperson.

# *The Formula*

I knew I was onto something great. In time, I had a conversation with a former colleague who worked on the development of the charitable software platform. I brought him up to speed on the experiment and told him that I was implementing a sales process that was highly effective. As I tweaked my process, I kept score and soon realized that it was drastically improving my closing ratios. I told him that my process in this industry could increase closing ratios with qualified prospects significantly. We discussed what impact that could have on this industry if it could be effectively taught.

As I executed the multiple steps of my process, I realized that if they were performed correctly, ultimately I would get the desired result: the sale. With additional scrutiny, I recognized that each phase of the process fell under one of the three clearly identifiable sections. The three parts and the multiple subsections represented a specific method of doing something to achieve a particular end—a formula. *That* is why I've put together this book … to share this method to help you achieve success! Of course, before putting this in writing, I needed to test, retest, tweak, and use this formula in a variety of roles to determine if it could be applied to any industry with the same results. I'm happy to report that yes, it can:

*Relate, Reason, Resolve = Results!*

I realized that knowing this formula and understanding each element of the underlying process was sales dynamism.

I soon accepted a position as a regional director of sales for another company in the senior housing industry, where I supervised a team of salespeople. All the assumptions about the improvement opportunities were made clear once I began working with my team. I started to teach them what I had developed during my experiment, and I realized that to improve significantly, they needed consistent training. I asked myself, *How I can teach my salespeople these concepts progressively?* I held a weekly training session over the phone, which lasted only ten to fifteen minutes, and as my team began to implement the processes I immediately saw an increase in closing ratios. Although this process materialized during my involvement with senior housing sales, I quickly realized that it could be adapted to any product or service that is sold.

*R3R1: The Sales Formula for Success* is about connecting a series of small and large ideas to create a better process. This process would be comparable to a football team and their playbook. Some of the plays are quite simple: run the ball between the tackle and the guard, straight up the middle. Others are quite complicated: the flea flicker, the double reverse, or the screen. Some of the best coaches script their first ten or twenty plays to include a mix of simple and complicated plays. Using a series of processes within the framework of *relating, reasoning,* and *resolving* to win the sale and get *results* is what *R3R1: The Sales Formula for Success* involves. So, I encourage you to keep reading until you see all the plays unfold into the R3R1 sales process.

# R3R1—THE SALES FORMULA FOR SUCCESS

# R3R1

R3R1 transfers to all sales situations and results in what every business is trying to achieve —*increased sales!*

## R3R1:

Relate, Reason, Resolve = Results

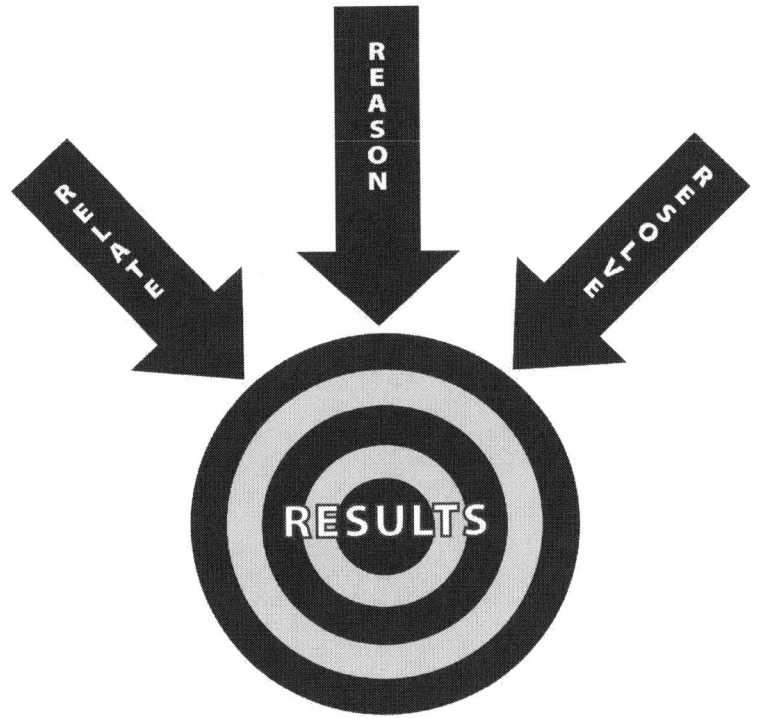

This formula is designed to assist you by helping you improve your messaging, sales strategy, and performance at all points of the sales process. Using it will improve performance, which in turn will increase overall profitability.

I developed the formula and derivative sales process over a period of years. Initially, I scripted an original sales process beginning with a series of individual steps. After each sales presentation, I would evaluate my performance by conducting a post-mortem review—something all successful salespeople should do. I would scrutinize each step in the performance and contemplate the reaction of the prospect, revising the presentation to increase my effectiveness in communicating key concepts. During this process, I confirmed that I was closing an increasingly higher percentage of prospects.

As revisions progressed, the number of steps in my presentation grew. I evaluated the results when I may have forgotten to follow a step, or if I had changed up the sequence during my presentations. Eventually, I realized that the entire sales process could be divided into three main categories: relating, reasoning, and resolving. By creating these main categories, I made the process much easier. It just makes sense that it's simpler to recall and manage three steps instead of dozens! Everything eventually boiled down to this:

- Did I relate with the prospect?
- Did I reason with the prospect?
- Did I resolve the issues that were important to the prospect?

If I accomplished all three of these points, the results became apparent—higher closing rates. Now, let's take a moment to dig into what I mean when I say relate, reason, and resolve, so we're all on the same page.

## *Relate*

A critical part of the sale occurs right when the salesperson first meets a prospect. The warm-up starts with the first hello, regardless of the business transaction taking place or what is being sold. That initial meet-and-greet is where the relationship begins.

What it comes down to is this—people prefer to do business with those they trust. It's human nature that if we can't *relate* with someone, a trust level, a bond, is not going to develop. This bond of trust develops the more we learn about the person as well as how much they get to know us.

Genuinely get to know your prospect as a person. Relating is one of the most important parts of the sales process! Miss this step, and you've started an uphill battle that is rarely won.

It is important to think about the impact this type of personal conversation with prospects has in a sales situation. Any time a salesperson is talking with a new prospect, he should consciously think of the discussion as an integral part of the *warm-up section* of the sales process. The longer he talks to the prospect about non-business issues, about their lives and their interests, the warmer the relationship becomes. Have you ever done business on a golf course? If not, the unwritten rule of business-golf is that you don't talk about business until the seventh hole. Why? For the same reasons I mention above. If the approach is simply to get down to business, the prospect is making a cold business decision, and you're struggling against the wind. By doing things this way, you're making it very easy for a prospect to say no to you, and since there's no relationship, there's not much to lose! If you pay attention to the warm-up portion of the sales presentation, it will directly increase your sales results.

## Reason

The skill of *reasoning* with prospects is equally crucial to establishing the initial relationship. Closely associated with reasoning is persuading—which is often linked to selling. However, selling is transacting business, and before anyone is buying anything there needs to be considerable reasoning. Prospects must be reasoned with on any number of issues during the sales process to reach a conclusion—the sale.

The idea of reasoning with someone is at the core of what great salespeople do. During the reasoning section of a presentation, there are usually many points, and each is important to reason out the issues with the prospect.

## Resolve

You must be able to resolve the obstacles or issues that are preventing your customer from making a commitment. That is why *resolve* is the third aspect of the sales formula for success. If a salesperson has excellent personal skills and can relate with customers and can reason with them, but lacks the ability to resolve their concerns, it's obvious that it will impact their sales negatively. The inability to address spoken *and* unspoken objections adversely affects the outcome of the sale.

## Results

At the end of the formula of success is the *result*. Is there anything more important in business than sales results? If your answer was anything but an emphatic no, then you've not been under a sales goal before! Sales, in its purest and simplest form, is all about results. Just like in sports, a win is better than a loss, even if it was an ugly win. But, just like in sports, you can't survive long on ugly wins. That's why you're reading this book right now. You want to turn ugly wins into smooth wins and losses into *more* wins!

The result that business owners and managers want is for qualified prospects to buy their product or service. You sell more, the company does better, you make more money, your clients are happy—and when you win, everyone wins.

Now, as promised, I am going back to the pig story! It wasn't until many years later that I understood the significance of that entire event and why I wound up not getting any donuts that day. It finally clicked why my father was so upset. Simply put, one of his twenty prospects jumped out of the trailer and was lost forever. My dad knew the exact amount of money he had invested in getting each pig, each qualified prospect, to the stockyard, and all he saw that day was his hard-earned money jump out of the back of his trailer and make a dash for freedom. As a kid, I thought the whole event was hilarious. As a seasoned sales professional, I saw it from a different set of eyes. Perhaps when I was a child, I didn't view my father as a seasoned sales professional, but in his way, he was. He saw the cost and the value of everything he did.

Ask yourself: how many pigs are jumping out of *your* trailer? Obviously, you are aware of the customer acquisition costs. You know that qualified prospects are not free. My father had 5 percent of his business jump out of the truck, and he became unglued. Let's say you are very efficient and close 40 to 50 percent of the qualified prospects who contact your business. If you were a farmer driving his pigs to the stockyard and ten or more of your pigs just jumped out of the trailer, would you be okay with that?

I am not going to emphasize how you should increase activity and keep track of this activity using a "CRM" system with prospects who have already decided not to buy your product or service. I am not going to explain how you should advertise and market your product or service to capture new prospects. Make no mistake, these are important sales fundamentals—but there are plenty of other resources out there to tell you how to do that. My goal is to get you in tune with the strategies of what to do with *every* prospect you receive so you can make the most of it.

I am all about the opportunity at hand. When you are on the phone or meeting face-to-face with a qualified prospect, can you persuade the prospect to buy your company's product or service?

Every business has the same goal: increase conversions. However, there is evidence that some salespeople convince prospects *not* to use their company's product or service. Perhaps the prospect had some interest, but after talking to the salesperson, they decide not to buy.

What if you could get more prospects to buy your product or service? That is what *R3R1: The Sales Formula for Success* is all about—increasing conversion at the point of sale. The R3R1 formula will improve all other aspects of the business, including how you use your advertising dollars. As closing percentages increase, customer acquisition costs decrease. When sales conversions are higher, every aspect of the business is better, especially top-line revenue and net profits. The oft-repeated quote, "Nothing ever happens until a salesperson sells something," has been credited to more than one individual—no doubt in part because it is the foundation of business. Business and sales are tantamount—without a sale of a product or service, there is no business.

Above I've listed the components of the R3R1 formula: *relate, reason, resolve*. Let's get a thorough understanding of these elements. What makes them up? How do you work through them? How do you improve? The next chapters will walk you through it all.

## RELATE

- make a connection
- have or establish a relationship
- interact
- respond, especially favorably

ow does one effectively relate with a client or prospect? To accomplish this, you must do the following:

- Make a connection
- Build and establish a solid relationship
- Effectively and positively interact
- Respond favorably

Simple enough, right? Not so! Building trust is a complicated task, but I like to focus on concrete steps and points of understanding that lead to accomplishing the goal of successfully relating.

This section gives attention to each aspect of relating and helps you understand how it affects the outcome of the sales process. You will see how much of an impact first impressions can have on whether a prospect likes you. You will also learn how your initial encounter will determine whether *you* like an individual well enough as a qualified prospect to justify the investment of your time to deliver the sales presentation.

The goal of this section is to help you focus on how each facet of relating impacts the sales process and your ultimate success in doing business with your prospects.

At the end of the day, our effectiveness at relating influences our success as salespeople.

## *First Impressions*

Before we jump into these challenges, I'd like to share my thoughts on first impressions. I'm sure you've heard the saying "You never get a second chance to make a first impression." Honestly, without a positive first impression, the rest of the sales process could be made moot!

The first interaction with a prospect can set the stage for a good encounter or a bad one. We know that our prospects are making decisions about us immediately. We always want to do everything we can to reduce anything that could negatively bias the prospect. It could be anything from how we dress, the tidiness of our desk, or the cleanliness of the lobby or reception area of the building where we work. There's any number of first impression factors that we could include here, but the point is that many different things make first impressions.

Here's an example of this kind of first impression bias that occurred with me. I had a rather large, western-style mustache—your typical Wyatt Earp–looking thing, but not quite that big. Also, I have been known for wearing a bowtie. On first meeting with a prospect, he said to me, "Never trust a man in a bowtie with a mustache." Yeah … that was a big blow to any opportunity I thought I had to sell this individual. He had some predisposition against people who wear bowties and have mustaches. Oddly, he voiced his opinion out loud.

Now, you might think, "Well, that's his hang-up," or "That was utterly stupid behavior on his part." All that may be true, but it didn't change the fact that he was the one I wanted to sell!

I would never do something that knowingly prejudiced my prospect against me. It so concerned me that after that meeting, I went directly to the Internet and looked this up to see if it was a common saying. I could not find anything that connected bowties and mustaches with distrust, and this was the only time I had ever heard such a saying. I attributed the incident to a family tale that perhaps was passed down and not something widely accepted. Let me assure you that if I had found out that this was a legitimate viewpoint, I would have shaved or changed to a straight necktie.

(By the way, I did not make the sale to him because we could not relate, and he did not trust me when I tried to reason with him—no surprise.)

The moral of the story is probably obvious—we don't want to *knowingly* prejudice any prospect against ourselves.

# *The Warm-Up*

Okay, enough of story time. I think you get the point that before any of these steps can occur, you need to do all you can to assure that your first impressions are good ones. Let's work from the assumption that your first impression was incredible and that things are looking good for you. Now we move onto the warm-up.

There are so many instant methods available today to communicate with people: email, text messaging, and social media platforms, such as Instagram, Facebook, Twitter, and Snapchat. Day-to-day routines have become fast-paced.

Depending on your industry, prospects may want to get down to business and immediately discuss the product or service or deliverables. They may be giving you the impression that liking you is not a factor if you have the product or service they are seeking. The problem is that is not at all true. The person is far less likely to buy from you if they do not like you or trust you because they have the predisposition toward bias. So what can we do about this situation? If possible, have the prospect spend some time getting to know you, so that they will trust you. Under some circumstances, this simply won't be possible, but in most sales situations, you can take some time to engage in small talk with the prospect to get to know them and help them get to know you.

I have been asked by sales teams how much time to spend on small talk during the sales process. My answer is as long as the prospect will allow! If you converse with the individual for fifteen or twenty minutes—or more—before you get into the next steps of the sales process, so what?

What is the hurry, especially if that time is the difference between someone buying from you or not? As I've stated before, people do business with people they like and trust. Even if the prospect will only spend a few minutes relating, that is still good. Perhaps you made an instant connection.

The problem is that many sales professionals are not even trying to relate to their prospects. In many cases, the salesperson questions the individual about themselves, which can be like an interrogation session. You want your discussion to flow back and forth like a normal conversation where you are trying to get to know a new friend. Realistically, you are not going to become lifelong friends; you are only trying to establish rapport and trust.

Sometimes a prospect is not going to want to have this type of dialogue at all and will become irritated if you try to engage in small talk. If this is the case, I typically move my process along and finish my qualifying, answer questions, and engage in some initial reasoning. However, if I get a chance, I will re-introduce small talk and revert to the warm-up with the prospect. This method works nearly all the time. I have found that if I cannot return to the warm-up session, I rarely, if ever, close the sale. I once had a prospect who became so irritated with me and said "Show me what you got!" so I started to reason with him. He then demanded that I talk about the product. So, I fast-forwarded to the deliverable portion of my process. I then attempted to build a relationship again, and he willingly went along. Next, I reviewed my reasoning points, and he went along as well. Then I went through my resolving process and closed the sale. I did not think for a moment that I could abandon the relating and reasoning part of my process and have any hope of doing business with this gentleman. I would have lost the sale.

As was mentioned earlier, if you pepper a prospect with one question after another without sharing any details about yourself, you are an interrogator. Take some time and tell them about yourself. Some of the things I like to share about myself are stuff like where I am from: *"a farm in Kansas … have you ever been to Kansas?"* After learning about the prospect's family, I may mention my family: *"I have been married to Kathleen for thirty-four years, and we have had two children."* I may talk about my hobbies: *"I love to play the drums … do you play an instrument?"* Perhaps the discussion involves travel: *"Oh, you are originally from South Dakota? I have been there several times … I love Spearfish Canyon."* Since I have traveled extensively, it certainly builds camaraderie if I can relate an adventure that I experienced during a visit to their hometown. All of this helps my prospect get to know me so that I am not just another salesperson trying to sell them something.

So what is the point? When it is your turn to tell your story, tell it and build a relationship with your prospect.

## Qualifying Prospects

Prospect

Can afford your product or service

Meets your demographics

Is willing to meet with you on a favorable basis

# *Qualifying Prospects*

Before you can begin the process of relating, reasoning, and resolving, it is imperative that you determine if you are dealing with a qualified prospect. Only after this determination has been made can you move on to the sales process. Why is this key to the process? There are only a certain number of hours in the workday, and time is capital. To spend time with an unqualified prospect is throwing away your principal asset. If you are trying to earn commissions, you need to make sure you are not delivering detailed presentations or pursuing unqualified candidates.

Who is a prospect? The following criteria must be met for an individual to meet the definition that I endorse:

- A prospect can afford to buy what I am selling.
- A prospect meets my demographics.
- A prospect is willing to meet with me on a favorable basis.

First, if the person cannot afford your product, you are done. There is no reason to proceed to the next step.

Second, the person meets your demographics. This is an industry-specific qualifier. Every business should know the demographics of their core customers. For example, the demographic for the customer of an off-road motorcycle is probably not a sixty-five-year-old male. Is the person who uses your product male or female? If applicable, is your location convenient?

Lastly, will they meet with you on a favorable basis? Let's take a moment to make sure you precisely understand what I mean, because not understanding it can be an enormous potential time-waster.

Here is an example: Some individual calls you on the phone and says that she is thinking about buying something from you. During your initial call, you determine that she can afford the purchase and meets your demographics. So, you ask to make an appointment, and she will not commit to scheduling an appointment to meet. You call five more times, and she never returns your call. Is she a qualified prospect? No, because she will not meet with you on a favorable basis. Stop chasing this person and move on to someone who has a legitimate interest.

It is important to qualify an individual as quickly as possible without them knowing you are doing it. Your success is contingent on time spent closing qualified prospects and not on time spent with non-prospects. Remember, your time is your most valuable asset.

## *Answering Questions*

Answering questions seems uncomplicated—the prospect asks something that you can easily answer, and you rattle off the details. However, before you jump right into that dialogue, it is important to recognize that *when* and *how* we respond to questions can increase sales conversions. Questions provide insight into the mindset of an individual and help you understand where someone is in the buying process. Ask enough questions, and your prospect will tell you how they want to be sold!

Can you control the question-and-answer portion of the presentation? Yes, to some degree. Think about this: If you have already developed a good rapport during the relating stage of your process, before answering their questions, what you say will be more readily accepted. This person may now like and trust you. On the other hand, if you have not had an opportunity during the warm-up to relate to the individual, they might be suspect of anything you say. Answering questions before a connection is established may be unavoidable. However, you should return to relating if possible.

After you have spent enough time relating with someone, then it makes sense to initiate questions, and that starts with the simple phrase: "What questions do you have for me?"

Prospects may ask you questions even if they have asked them previously, perhaps during an initial phone conversation. The best questions for taking a prospect's temperature are the ones they ask us. We want them to ask questions freely, and we want to answer them in ways that commit them to buy our product or service.

Recognize the opening that presents itself during the question-and-answer process, which can influence the sale. You can create a commitment opportunity by answering *with* a question.

> Q: "What color does this car come in?"
> A: "What colors do you like?"
>
> Q: "Do I have to replace all of the windows in my home at one time?"
> A: "If we could arrange it where you could replace a few at a time, would you be more likely to move forward?"
>
> Q: "Can I get a (back massage, ride to the bar, lobster dinner, etc.) once a week at your retirement community?"
> A: "If we could arrange that, would you move in?"

These are just a few examples of using a question to answer a question with the goal of gaining additional insight into the thought process, as well as getting *mini* commitments from the prospect.

Being effective at using questions takes practice, but with time you can become very efficient at it. You must become comfortable with questions and be prepared to provide answers that include well-structured questions.

# *The Why*

When you are speaking with a potential prospect, one of the most important things you can understand is what is motivating them to consider your product. There are a couple of reasons that this is important. First, it helps you identify a genuine prospect. Second, it enables you to reason on and resolve the priority issues.

To determine whether an individual is a prospect and identify the reasons they are inquiring (the *why* of it all), here is an example of a probing question that will get you the answer you need:

*"Why are you considering our product?"*

One response might be, "I was just shopping next door and thought I'd stop in to see what you do here." Obviously, an individual that says something like this is probably not a prospect that you would devote valuable time with delivering a full sales presentation.

Another typical response could go as follows, "Oh, I am just considering this. I am not sure if I am ready to switch to a SuperSuction model quite yet." With this type of response, you determine that the prospect may be guarded and not mention specific solutions that they are in search of, seeking information and not wanting to speak freely.

Perhaps the reply to your question is, "Well, my carpet never seems clean enough. I think my current model isn't working right, and my friend has a SuperSuction, and I like the way that it performs." Perhaps a good prospect here, as they are freely sharing some additional information and telling you what's important to them.

When the prospect explains why they are seeking your solution, this provides an opportunity to develop a strategic line of reasoning. How will using your product provide a solution? Aligning to this will significantly improve your chances of closing the sale.

When you ask the *why* question, listen intently for the answer. It's imperative that you clear your mind of anything else happening during your conversation and focus on what the person is saying. Let the prospect talk if they want to. If I am on the phone with someone and ask them the *why* question, I close my eyes and try to listen as intently as I can. When they finish telling me, I take detailed notes and refer to them in preparation for our next meeting.

When should you ask the *why* question? Although it should be as soon as possible, I like to wait until I have spent time relating with the prospect before I ask them. I want the prospect to feel comfortable sharing with me what is motivating them so that I can adjust other sections of my presentation by emphasizing features that they want from my product.

If we know *why* the prospect is contacting us, we can dial into their core motives. It seems simple, but it isn't. Finding out the *why* is critical to the sale process. I cannot even imagine dealing with a prospect and not attempting to find out the *why*—and neither should you.

# *Insurmountable Obstacles*

Another crucial reason to follow these steps is to find those that in fact might not be a prospect (even after your relating) because you will be hit with the occasional insurmountable obstacle.

Early on in your presentation, it is critical to determine if there are grounds to halt the sales process. At times, insurmountable barriers cannot be reasoned through or resolved by the best salesperson in the world, so you need to identify them as soon as you can. It is imperative that you do not waste time with someone who is never going to buy your product or service. Remember, prospects do not qualify themselves—that is your job. So, it is important that you determine basic guidelines for *ending* a presentation.

Develop a few probing questions to uncover insurmountable obstacles. If you ignore these obstacles, you will waste a lot of time with non-prospects who will never buy from you. Here are two typical examples from two different industries:

*Example One: Senior Housing*

Most seniors want to move into a retirement community within ten miles of where they currently live or where their adult children live. A shrewd salesperson will always ask, "How does our location work for you and your family?"

Even though the prospect has inquired about the community, they may not have thought through this issue. However, when questioned, the potential resident will say things like, "I would never live in this area—it is too far from my church" (or doctor, favorite store, etc.). Or the family might say, "Your location is quite a distance from my home, and that would make it hard for me to visit my mom as often as I want."

It sounds like this is a dead deal, but make sure you have a follow-up question ready to go for verification, such as, "So, you're saying that even if our community fits all your needs, you won't choose us based on the location. Is that correct?"

The prospect says, "Yes, that is correct." What is the point of continuing this presentation? The wrong location is a deal killer. There is no sale—it is an insurmountable obstacle, and it's time for the smart salesperson to move on.

*Example Two: Car Sales*

A prospect steps onto the showroom floor at the local Fiat dealership and expresses interest in one of the latest models. When the salesperson questions him, he indicates that he can afford a payment around $600 a month.

He mentions that he wants to do something right away, so the salesperson starts to show him some cars. He explains all the features and even takes him on a test drive without probing to find out about his personal situation. An hour or so later, they return to the dealership, and the salesperson finally learns that his prospect has a wife and five small children—a family of seven! Seven people cannot fit in even the largest model that the salesperson has to offer. A simple question like "How are you going to use this car?" would have smoked out this insurmountable obstacle, but instead, the salesperson spent two hours of his time and missed another sale. Lesson: If you sell tiny cars, you might want to inquire how many people will be riding in the car.

The point is simple. The right questions will lead you in the right direction—either to closing a sale or closing the door to the sale. Either way, you're making the most of your valuable time so you can spend it on those that have a chance to close!

## REASON

- think through logically
- conclude or infer
- convince, persuade by reasoning
- an explanation of a situation or circumstance which made certain results seem possible or appropriate

The next portion of our formula is *reasoning*. Let's define this segment. To *reason* is to:

- Think through things logically
- Conclude or infer
- Convince or persuade by reasoning
- Explain a situation or circumstance which makes certain results seem possible or appropriate

As with *relating*, there are many opportunities throughout the sales cycle to reason with your prospect and get a solid understanding of what it will take to reason with them effectively. As before, let's take a moment to get a solid understanding of the *foundation of reasoning* and some of the challenges and roadblocks faced, so we're all on the same page.

In addition to laying a foundation, some of the points in the reasoning section that you will learn to incorporate in each of your sales presentations include facts about your company and its mission. You will see how details about your customers' experiences and the suitability of your product or service for certain demographics of the market can be an influential factor during your presentation. You will also learn how to incorporate other key messages, which when delivered at the right time during your process will ultimately help you close more sales.

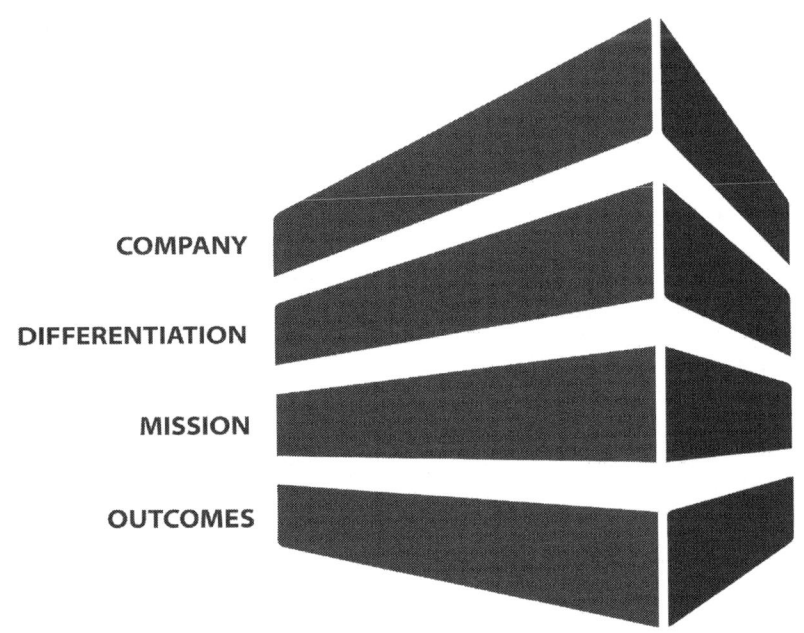

# *Foundation of Reasoning*

If I were asked what is the most important thing that someone can take away from this book, my first response would be to try to use as much of the entire process as you can absorb and execute. I know how important all the steps of the process are; however, the area that I see as the weak spot is that of *reasoning*.

In my experiences over the years, when I am either buying something or training salespeople, I have listened to numerous presentations and have rarely seen anyone properly reason with me. Not reasoning effectively with prospects results in closing far fewer sales, since you are not giving the candidate sound reasons to buy.

In sales, it is our job to convince someone to use our product. However, it is bizarre that no salesperson that has tried to sell me anything has ever made a reasonable argument. If I haven't already decided to buy the product on my own, I usually give the salesperson an excuse (the smokescreen), end the meeting, and never buy their product. Often, the truth is that I was *somewhat* interested in buying the product until I talked to the salesperson, and then he talked me out of being interested because he never gave me the reasons to buy.

Most salespeople can relate with a prospect, as well as resolve issues like the budget, product selection, suitability, and delivery. However, very few salespeople know how to reason effectively with prospects, and this is at the core of selling.

Imagine a lawyer who is polished, affable, and well-spoken. He delivers his closing argument, helping the jury resolve what they should do with his client. The only problem is that he never reasoned with the jury on why his client was in the right. He made no arguments! That is what most salespeople are doing when they do not reason with their prospects; they are not making a logical argument.

The reasoning section of the sales process is its foundation. Without it, your house (presentation) is built on sand and will not withstand the prospect's scrutiny, risk concerns, conscious and unconscious thoughts, and unspoken objections and questions.

So, let's review the fundamentals of reasoning and what is accomplished by using them in every sales situation.

1. Tell your prospect about the company you work for and why they should have trust and confidence in the company.
2. Explain to your prospect why your product or service is different from your competition.
3. Discuss with the prospect how your company's mission is in sync with *their* goals as it relates to your product.
4. Demonstrate through statistics and specific reasoning points the fact that your customers have a better outcome and experience using your product or service.

You should know how to deliver that presentation in less than two minutes (speed messaging) on the phone or in a brief face-to-face interaction. You should be able to give a longer version (ten to fifteen minutes) on demand, during the reasoning section of your full presentation.

A multi-layered reasoning presentation is so powerful it is almost hard to describe. If you learn your reasoning points, practice them and deliver them consistently, it will elevate your salesmanship to the next level.

# Company Presentation

One of the most important things you can do is explain the company and what it's all about. Prospects are weighing the following options:

- Buying the product from your company
- Buying from a competitor
- Doing nothing (status quo)

Whenever someone is considering the purchase of an expensive item, they recognize and assume a certain amount of risk. In fact, many companies have entire departments dedicated to analyzing the risks of making certain purchases or investments. However, individual buyers also make those assessments—but they rely on themselves and perform the analysis either consciously or unconsciously.

Explaining the company's story is a vital part of your presentation, and skipping it may be to the detriment of the sale. You must convince the prospect that there is minimal risk in doing business with your company. Unfortunately, this is a silent sales killer. The prospect is not going to voice his concerns. If you are not covering this information during the presentation, you are the one that has the risk—of losing their business.

Even if you did a great job during the warm-up and you have related well with a prospect, that does not automatically mean that they trust your company. When buying a product, the prospect has to believe that the company providing the product is going to live up to their promises.

If the candidate does not believe in the company, then they are simply not buying.

You must include the story of your company and explain why your company is trustworthy and how it keeps its promises. All great companies have a story based on traditions and other virtues. For example, a well-known story is that of Sam Walton and Walmart. The first Walmart was in Rogers, Arkansas. As Walmart grew, Sam Walton remained committed to making sure that his customers would always get a good value. In fact, if you look at their website, it states that they are "committed to providing low prices every day, on everything." And if that is not enough of a compelling story, it goes on to state that "if you find a lower price from an online retailer on an identical, in-stock product, or the item purchased from Walmart.com is now listed at a lower price, tell us, and we'll match it."

I am sure you can relate the history of other companies as easily. The reason you know their story is because they make sure you know it, so that you will trust them and do business with them. Some companies go to a lot of trouble, not to mention expense, to convey their story to build a solid customer base and overcome perceived risks of doing business.

When you communicate the story of your company, focus on building confidence. Don't assume that the prospect knows anything about your company or that they already trust you—they may not. One of the ways to introduce the company section of your presentation is to ask the prospect simply: "So, what do know about our company?"

The answer is probably going to be the same in most cases—"nothing." So, if you do not currently include a company section in your sales presentation, start today, and you will see your sales increase.

# *Differentiation Statements*

A well-designed sales presentation includes various differentiation statements, both straightforward and complex. It is not only important to highlight the differences between you and your competition, but also emphasize why someone should choose you. You must explain why the prospect should choose your product or service rather than the competition during each sales presentation.

Of course, you must whole-heartedly believe these statements and say them with conviction. A professional differentiation presentation, delivered with precision, will convince many prospects to select your offering without considering the competition. As you develop your presentation, describe select differences that will highlight the best qualities of your product. Include and explain in detail the reasons *why* the feature is different.

- Why are you different from your competition?
- Why was this product created?
- Why is your service delivered in a particular manner?

Comprehensive differentiation statements will have more of an impact than merely reciting product details.

*Example: Walking Trail*

"The company designed our retirement community with a quarter-mile walking trail around the entire property. The reason we created this walking trail is that we want our residents to feel compelled to walk around our community, to get needed exercise, and increase their overall enjoyment. It also provides our residents with an opportunity to socialize with each other. You may have noticed that the other communities in our area do not have custom-designed walking trails like ours."

Now think about what I just did with this statement. I used something as simple as a concrete sidewalk around a retirement community to create differentiation. You need to carefully study your offering, know your competition, and contemplate the differences, no matter how insignificant they may seem.

*Example: Tablecloths and Fresh Flowers*

"You may have noticed that in our dining room, we always set the tables with crisp white linen and vases with fresh-cut flowers. The reason is that we believe that dining is one of the most important aspects of living in our community. As we age, there are fewer things we can still enjoy, and eating is one source of pleasure for most seniors. We want our seniors to linger after the meal and socialize with the other residents. We want them to look forward to coming to the dining room and have an outstanding dining experience. If you have visited other communities in the area, you may have noticed that they do not have white tablecloths in their dining rooms. They may only have a paper placemat and a fake floral arrangement on the table. Such decor does not promote the fine dining experience we expect for our residents."

You need to consider what the competition may be saying at the other retirement community to differentiate his service. His dining room has no tablecloths and no fresh flowers, and he may have a compelling presentation to convince the prospect that this is a better arrangement.

*Example: No Tablecloths or Fresh Flowers*

"You may have noticed that our dining room does not have white tablecloths like some of the other communities in our area. Let me ask you a question. Do you eat off of a white tablecloth at home? No, I didn't think so. Well, we want you to be at home here at our community. We do not want to promote a stuffy atmosphere where you cannot relax like you would in your home."

Which one of those arguments is most appealing to you—the first statement *for* the tablecloths and flowers, the second statement *against* the tablecloths and flowers, neither statement, or both? Interestingly, the one that will influence the prospect the most is the one that is delivered consistently with belief and sincerity. Unfortunately, many sales professionals will not even include differentiation statements during a sales presentation, much less give them to their prospects.

Can you see the advantages in the sales presentation that highlights differences, describes benefits and why they make sense, and then explains why it is the best way to accomplish a specific deliverable or process?

# ALIGNING INTERESTS

## *Mission Statement*

A company's mission statement helps employees and customers understand the following:

- Who the company is
- What the company does
- What the company expects to accomplish

As the salesperson of the company, you must understand this mission and include a version of the mission statement within your sales presentation during the *reasoning* section.

Establishing and consistently delivering this message is highly effective when prospects are making the decision to buy from you. Again, the goal of the mission statement is to answer unspoken objections and reduce potential concerns the prospect may have about the risk of buying your product.

How do you adapt the mission statement for your sales presentation? If your company has a published mission statement, that is a good place to start. If they do not, you need to reflect on the objectives of your company and its overall goals.

The plan is to extract from your company's mission statements the elements that you are going to incorporate into your presentation. You must sincerely reflect on how the personal application of the statement affects your customers' use of the product. Next, you must consider how the mission affects the experience of the individual in using the product. Additionally, you need to determine how it impacts the financial value of your offering. The statement you put forth must be based on real facts, not hoped for outcomes.

The following point is the key to this process: Write a list of what you think your core prospect wants to accomplish when they inquire about your product. Coordinate your presentation, aligning the needs of the prospect with your company's mission.

Again, the mission statement is meant to help the prospective customer understand what your company is trying to accomplish, as well as how your company will help them reach their goals as they relate to the purchase and use of your product. The result is that the candidate believes that he will reach his anticipated goals because your company's mission is in sync with his desired outcome. When this alignment occurs, the prospect is much more likely to purchase your product.

*Example: Specialty Boat Builder*

This company builds solid mahogany boats by hand. These unique creations are replicas of the classic Runabout boats of the 1940s and '50s. Each handcrafted boat costs between $100,000 to $200,000. The company's mission is to build the most authentic solid mahogany boat with the highest possible quality materials and the best craftsmanship. Because the boat is built by hand, production is limited. Therefore, this is an exclusive boating experience that is available only to a privileged few.

The sales professional thinks about the mission of his company and takes into consideration his prospect's needs and desires. His customer is a financially well-heeled man who loves boating and wants to own an antique wood boat, but does not want to deal with the maintenance of owning a boat that is sixty years old or older. Additionally, he is looking for a prized possession of the highest quality that sets him apart in his circle of friends.

With his company's mission statement and product in mind, along with his prospects wish list, the salesperson composes the following statement: "Our mission as a company is to build the highest-quality solid mahogany Runabout with the finest materials and craftsmanship so that our customers can experience the pleasure of owning a brand-new solid mahogany wood boat fashioned after the Runabouts of the 1940s and '50s. Additionally, it is our mission to build a limited number of boats so that our owners can enjoy the benefits of having an exclusive boating experience."

Then he asks his prospect this question: "Is that what you are trying to accomplish?"

If the prospect says "Yes, that is what I am trying to achieve," the salesperson responds with, "You should buy my boat because we have the same goals."

Do you see the power of incorporating the mission within the presentation? It aligns the goals of the prospect with the goals of the company you represent. It helps eliminate unspoken objections and reduces the prospect's concerns about the risks involved with the purchase. It is one of the most powerful sales tools to increase conversion percentages if it is developed, practiced, and delivered consistently.

## *Outcomes*

Although a prospect may not express it aloud, the *outcomes section* of your presentation must answer the following question: "Why should I use your product or conduct business with your company?"

Think about it! If I am not going to have a better outcome using your product than not using it, then why should I buy it? You must clearly explain to your prospect that unquestionably they will have a far better outcome by using your product. You may even need to be prepared with available statistics that demonstrate that your customers are experiencing better outcomes than individuals that are not using your product.

There are various ways to explain why someone should use your service. However, focus on what your company is going to deliver through its offering and the outcome the prospect will have if they decide to use your service or product. Explain how your customers fare much better than individuals that do nothing or that buy from a competitor.

A simple statement, such as, "Our customers are faring much better than those who do not use our product or service," could elicit a response from the prospect. They may respond to your statement by asking, "Why is that?" This question opens the door for you to state your case using strong reasoning points based on well-researched facts.

*Example: Replacement Windows*

"There are many reasons why our customers have better outcomes since installing our windows. Our customers have reported that their homes are warmer and less drafty in the winter and are cooler in the summer. Therefore, they have consistently seen reduced heat and electric bills since installing the replacement windows."

The prospect may ask the following question: "Why are these windows having such an impact on their utilities?"

You can use this as an opportunity to explain the reasons why your product is superior: "This is because of the dual-pane glass and durable strength vinyl that we use when we custom-build our windows to fit your home. The double pane eliminates annoying outside sounds and does not require any maintenance, and our tilt mechanism makes the windows easy to clean. However, one of the most significant results from installing our replacement windows is that utility bill savings are reported to be between 7 and 15 percent because that dual-pane glass keeps the cold out and warmth in."

In addition to explaining outcomes, it is also important to discuss your prospect's needs, which will provide another opportunity for you to reinforce the reasons that they will have a better outcome using your product.

Ask yourself this question: "Do my prospective customers know why they should purchase this product?"

Do not rely on the prospect to ask the right questions. If you have not thoroughly explained the reasons why they will have a better outcome using your product or service, the prospect will never tell you that you have failed to help them understand why they should buy. They simply won't buy from you!

If you omit the *outcomes section* of your presentation, this will most likely be the result: "I am going to think about this and get back to you." Which, when translated, means they are not going to do anything because you have not articulated an improved outcome.

Surprisingly, some salespeople ignore this part of the presentation. Imagine how it will impact your results if you spend a reasonable amount of time with the prospect explaining why they should use your product.

## SPEED MESSAGING

## *Speed Messaging*

Understanding speed messaging is all well and good, but at some point, you're going *deliver* it in the right way.

There are a number of ways to deliver your message—and no shortage of books, webinars, seminars, and ideas on how to do it. I wouldn't presume to create an extensive listing here, as I could easily fill another book with that information. So, since I just got done telling you how important first impressions are—and how they can make or break everything beyond that point—let's talk about your speed messaging or, as it is often referred to, your elevator pitch.

The idea behind this is simple. You need to effectively convey main points about your business in the amount of time that it would take to ride between floors in an elevator. You don't have much time, and you are aware that it is critical to get your key messages to an individual very quickly and precisely.

A salesperson will typically engage the qualified prospect on the phone before an initial face-to-face meeting. So, if you are talking to a qualified prospect on the phone but you have not been able to set up a meeting, it is a good idea to speed-message the prospect so that they will know the essentials about your company and your product. Speed messaging should set the stage for your next meeting. Then, when you are delivering your full presentation, you will review these points again and expand on the key points of your message.

Speed messages must contain an abbreviated version of the following information:

- The company
- Differentiation statement
- Mission statement
- Outcomes

Speed messaging needs to be quick and consistent. The entire message should be delivered with *precision* in a matter of two minutes or less.

If you are not including speed messaging as part of your sales process, you want to start now. First, outline the core message that you want to share with your core prospects. Next, work on making the points concise by practicing your speed message. Finally, keep track of your performance, and document when you deliver the speed message when talking with a core prospect. Verify that you are consistently incorporating speed messaging in your sales activities.

Your ability to effectively present speed messages will determine if your core prospects will agree to meet with you on a favorable basis, as well as ultimately respond to your offering.

# *The Expert*

When an individual makes an inquiry into your company's product or service, the expectation is that, as a representative of the company, you are an expert in your field. It is essential that you have all the answers to any questions that your prospect brings up and that you anticipate what subjects need to be discussed. Granted, you won't know everything about everything, so you need to be equally polished if you're hit with a question that you can't answer. It's okay to say "I don't know." Most prospects are fine with that. However, the words following "I don't know" will be the key. Say nothing more than that, and you've lost your credibility. Make something up, and you've lost your credibility. Keep it simple, as in: "That's a great question—one I haven't heard before. I will get back to you with an answer."

More importantly, you need to know why the product or service is designed the way it is and delineate how everything works. Therefore, to build confidence and trust, you must have a thorough understanding of your product or service, and the prospect must be convinced that you are an expert in your field.

*Your goal: Be the expert.*

Increase your knowledge by reading as much as you can about your industry, company, product, service, and competition. You are at a disadvantage if you do not know more about these matters than your potential customer knows. Interestingly, a personal experience I had recently as a potential new car customer included the following interchange:

> Me: "Does this car alert you with an alarm or bell when there is something behind you or you are approaching an object too closely?"
>
> Salesman: "No, it is not equipped with that feature."

Well, that was not a deal-breaker, and I bought the vehicle regardless. Now, imagine my surprise when the car began sounding an alarm as I approached too closely to another vehicle, a curb, or a person—to the front of my vehicle, to the rear, and even to the side! Not a day goes by that I don't hear the familiar *beep, beep, beep,* and not a beep goes by that I don't think about the salesman at the dealership that didn't know his product had this feature!

Will I ever buy a vehicle from this same person again? Perhaps. But what is the likelihood that I would if the response had been "I'm not sure … let me find out right now," and he gave me the right answer?

Recognize what your operations team is doing to manage the business. It is to everyone's benefit if marketing and operations work together harmoniously. As the salesperson, do what you can to align interests with your operations team.

Understand the delivery process. You are selling a product or service that must be delivered. Know the details:

- Delivery cycle time
- Approval process
- Payment for goods or services
- Implementation/installation
- Build-out
- Physical delivery

Be familiar with the financial operations of the business. When you understand the finances of the business—what it takes to operate the business, top-line revenue, expenses, profit and loss statements—you will be able to defend pricing to prospects. Having this understanding gives you the authority to ask for money needed to keep the business profitable. You cannot be detached from the fact that the company you represent is a for-profit business, and to continue operating it needs to make money. Your success is tied to the financial well-being of the business.

To put it more succinctly, by making an investment of your time to increase your knowledge of the areas of your business, you will speak with authority and gain the confidence of your prospective customer.

# *The Unconscious Mind*

> *"The conscious mind determines the actions; the unconscious mind determines the reactions; and the reactions are just as important as the actions."*
> —E. Stanley Jones (1884–1973)

All your interactions with prospects need to be analyzed to determine how the prospect is evaluating you both consciously and unconsciously. The following areas can leave a lasting impression on the unconscious mind of an individual:

- How you dress
- Your office and meeting place
- The handshake
- Offering refreshments
- Providing clear answers to questions
- How well you listen
- Posted signs
- Showing alternative options
- Marketing materials
- Giving a small gift or token of appreciation

Your environment and everything that you do affect the individual's brain. Consider the following examples:

*Posted Sign: Out of Order*

When you see a sign posted on a piece of equipment that states that the item is "out of order," you may shrug it off and just use the next machine. However, at a deeper level, you may unconsciously be wondering, "How long has that machine been broken? When is it going to be repaired? Is this business having financial difficulties?"

*Posted Sign: Come On In*

Recently, my wife and I went to a familiar place of business and noticed that the office door was closed, and there was a typed-up sign on a sheet of paper that stated, "Come on in." We did not go into the office. It wasn't until a week later that we talked about it and both of us had the same conclusion. The door was shut, and that meant *keep out*, not *come on in*.

What messages are you sending to your potential customers? No detail is too minor to ignore, so be sure to thoroughly examine the signals you are sending, and you will avoid negative results.

## YES, MAYBE, NO

# YES = YES

# MAYBE = NO

# NO = NEXT

# *Yes, Maybe, No*

All of us like to win the sale. We like to hear "Yes, we are moving forward." We don't want to hear "No," but unfortunately this is something that all salespeople must accept.

What do you do when the prospect says no? You may not understand why the qualified candidate said no. So, you persist a while longer, thinking that the prospect could be persuaded into changing his mind and eventually saying yes.

What about when the prospect says maybe? Many salespeople think a *maybe* is like a *yes* when it is a *no*.

Unfortunately, the *maybe* is far worse than the *no* because it leaves hope in the heart of the salesperson that the prospect is planning on buying your service when they are not.

### *The China Egg Syndrome*

*The china egg looks like a real egg, but it is made of porcelain. No matter how long the hen sits on a china egg, it will not hatch.*

You may think that you have a qualified prospect, but it is a china egg, and the *maybe* causes you to sit around waiting for something to happen that never does.

Here is the solution: If the prospect tells you maybe, then remember the definition of *maybe*. In sales, the definition of *maybe* is *no*. It is not *yes*. When someone says yes, they are writing you a check.

This approach saves a lot of time and frustration. You will increase sales by closing qualified prospects, not wasting your time with people who have already decided not to buy from you.

Remember, if a prospect says "No," you say "Next," meaning bring on the next qualified prospect to give your next presentation. If they say "Maybe," you say "Next," because *maybe* means *no*.

# *The Smokescreen*

In a sales situation, many consumers believe (either consciously or unconsciously) that it is acceptable to lie to the salesperson. Why? Because being sold something is like a battle in that there is an inherent conflict. Can I just *look* at the product without the salesperson selling it to me? Therefore, to level the playing field, the prospect may employ the smokescreen.

> *Smokescreen: An action or statement used to conceal actual plans or intentions.*

So, what's the problem? The customer lies ... so what? Why are we discussing this at all? It is because you need to be prepared for the individual to tell little lies or to put up a smokescreen to throw you off track. You need to be alert for this kind of noise and stick with your presentation. If you become aware that a prospect is fibbing to you, just assume they are doing it as a defense mechanism and move on. Never confront them with any of the information about the untruth; just act as if they did not say it and move on. Your job is not to hold people accountable for what they say. Your job is to sell them your product or service.

Early on in my sales career, I was working as an automobile salesperson at a dealership in Wichita, Kansas. It was January, and we had a record of thirty days in a row where the actual temperature never reached zero. A gentleman came onto the lot, and when he walked into the showroom I asked him if he was looking for two doors, four doors, or a station wagon. (This is because I was selling new Volvos, and that what I had.)

He said, "Well, I am just looking today. I wanted to see what you had." Did I believe him? No! I never believed him for one second. I knew this guy was out to buy a car—why else would someone be out on a day when the wind chill was twenty below zero? Two hours later, as I was switching the tag from his old car to his new Volvo, I was glad I had the good sense to pull it into the shop.

Too often, salespeople will label a person who tells them that they "just want to look around" as tire kickers. Is that so? Maybe the prospect is seriously considering the purchase, but when approached, they attempt to distract the salesperson with a decoy statement. The salesperson bought the story, characterized the prospect as a tire kicker, and made no effort to sell the candidate. The potential customer subsequently leaves that business, goes to another, and meets a salesperson not distracted by the smokescreen and makes the intended purchase one hour later.

Do not let distractions or smokescreens derail your sales presentation. Phrases like "I'm just looking around" or "Let me think about it" or "I need to speak with my adviser" are nothing more than smokescreens.

Just assume that some part of the story you are being told is fabricated. Do not take it personally when this happens; the smokescreen is just the natural human reaction to stress when a person is purchasing an item and should transact business with a salesperson. The smokescreen is so common that even in the most complex sales situations, experienced salespeople come to expect it and do not take it personally.

# *Liars*

Google the phrase "salesmen are liars," and you will come up with at least 128,000 results. I have been in sales and marketing, either as a salesperson or a sales manager or business owner, for many years, and when I hear this remark, I am typically offended. At the very least, I'm annoyed. The fact is, only dumb salespeople are liars; the smart ones have a lot of integrity. Lying to your customers is a quick path to nowhere. When a salesperson lacks integrity, it affects the individual's experience, which affects the reputation and success of the entire business.

Some salespeople try to get away with telling untruths; typically these lies are about the deliverables. If the prospect's expectations of what the deliverables are going to be and what they end up being are far from the same, the situation ends badly. Erroneously describing deliverables is not embellishing or exaggerating—it is lying, and it is unacceptable.

The customer's experience is influenced by the expectations that are set by the salesperson. When the salesperson paints a picture of a product or service that will *not* be delivered, the result is unhappy customers, unhappy operations teams, and a business poised for failure. Most salespeople who distort the truth about what they are selling won't be employed very long when the lies are exposed. It is always better for the salesperson and his organization to abide by the highest level of integrity.

Google the phrase "the truth comes out in the end," and you will come up with about 6,330,000 results. We must make sure that we are thoroughly familiar with the deliverables and make sure that what we are telling the customer is accurate. If we do not know the answer, it is usually best to ask the appropriate person in the operations department (typically the one that is going to deliver the service) before providing a semi-educated guess about it.

We need to keep in mind the experience that the prospect is going to have *after* they buy from us. If you met with an individual and, based on your questions during your initial discussions, you determined that they would have a bad experience using your product or service, would you still attempt to sell to them? There is an old proverb that describes the act of raking fire into your bosom. In other words, you are going to get burned. Remember that customer experience is everything. After the sale is when all of the information conveyed to the prospect intersects with the expectations of a new customer. If your product or service meets the set expectations, then you will increase the likelihood of having a happy consumer that will sing your praises and provide you with referrals.

# THE RELATING AND REASONING EFFECT

**As relating and reasoning increase, trust and confidence increases**

| Relating | Reasoning | Trust and Confidence |
|---|---|---|
|  |  |  |

**As relating and reasoning decrease, trust and confidence decreases**

| Relating | Reasoning | Trust and Confidence |
|---|---|---|
|  |  |  |

# *Suitability*

How does the distrust of a salesperson affect the sales process? A lot of individuals believe that salespeople are motivated to say anything, true or false, just to get a sale. They believe the salesperson does not care about them. As a rule, most salespeople ignore this assessment. They think that they can just press ahead without it affecting the outcome of their sale which is false. What if you can do something about this perception and reason with the prospect to convince them that you are different and they can trust you?

Overcoming distrust can be achieved through *relating, reasoning,* and *resolving*. During the R3 process, the seller must convince the buyer that he has their best interest at heart. One of the most important points that you must convey to the prospect during the reasoning and resolving phases of the sales process is that you do not want them to purchase your product or service if they are not going to have a good outcome.

If you are convinced that they are not going to have a positive outcome, you will refuse to sell them your product or service because it will only hurt them and you. Refusing to sell a prospect your product is not a matter of reverse psychology; it must be real. If, on principle, the salesperson refuses to sell his product or service to people who he believes will have an adverse outcome, this will gain him the highest level of credibility. It will allow him to get his qualified prospects to place their trust in him. If that kind of trust can be established in addition to a *liking* relationship, then real business can be conducted. The salesperson has been able to knock down a significant barrier to the prospect buying.

The concept is, "We want people to use our product or service who will have a good outcome."

A *good outcome* is a very simple yet powerful concept because people often purchase products and services and do not have a good experience. The customer's experience is the most important aspect. Real success is reliant on customer satisfaction.

Using suitability to approach the problem of distrust of salespeople will increase your sales substantially. You must reason with your prospect as to why you will only allow appropriate people to buy your product or service. You do not want unhappy customers, and so you do not sell to inappropriate people—period.

## *Commitment Questions*

As you proceed through each stage of your presentation—you have *related* with the prospect, discussing the company and why your product or service is different, as well as your company's mission, and you have explained that the prospect is going to have a better outcome using your product or service—once foundational *relating* and *reasoning* have taken place, it is a good idea to take the temperature of the prospect. You need to determine if there is buy-in to what you have been discussing. The best way to measure this is by asking a few viewpoint questions. These questions should be posed in such a way to understand what the prospect is thinking and if they are committed to the ideas you have been sharing with them.

Additionally, it's imperative to ask for commitments from the prospect before the end of the presentation. Here are a few examples taken from different industries:

*Insurance Agent*

"Would you like to make sure that your family has a secure future?" That question may seem uncomfortable to ask, but it is fundamental as it relates to life insurance. Of course, the answer will most likely be yes.

*Senior Housing*

Speaking to an adult child of a potential resident: "Would you like for your mom to be happier, healthier, and safer?" This viewpoint question can precipitate different responses. It may be a simple yes, or "I think she is pretty happy, healthy, and safe now—but she could always improve." What if the prospective resident's child answers the question as follows: "I don't care about her being happy, healthy, or safe." Apparently, that could indicate that the child does not care enough to make sure that his mom is living in a beneficial environment.

*Electric Car Sales*

"Aren't you looking forward to skipping the gas station and oil changes?" Purposely ask them a question that they can quickly answer yes to. You do not want *no* answers from your prospects. The goal is to condition the prospect to say *yes* repeatedly. Therefore, it is important to use commitment questions that are most likely going to illicit yes responses.

Just like so many other steps in a typical sales presentation, if you skip the pre-close or pre-commitment phase of the sales presentation—just because you have not created these questions or practiced them, or you forget to do it, or it makes you uncomfortable—you are losing sales. It is important to create, practice, and implement this strategy to get mini-commitments or buy-in from prospects before you are at the end of the presentation.

# *Why Logic*

An underlying theme that you may have noticed in the reasoning section as well as other parts of this book is to *explain the why* or to use *why logic*.

When you are reasoning with a prospect, you are developing logical arguments, and *why logic* is much more compelling than *what logic*. Explaining the *what* is done way too often in sales presentations, but the fact is that it's not even remotely as convincing as clarifying the *why*. Let's give consideration into how you can use *why logic*.

When you first meet a prospect and you are in the relating phase of the sales process, you can explain *why* you are the one that the prospect is meeting and *why* you are the person representing the company.

When you are reasoning with the prospect about your company, you can explain *why* the company exists in the first place. Most, if not all, companies have a "how we got started" story that is typically noteworthy and compelling.

Next, you'll have the discussion as to *why* your product or service is different. The *why* is a very powerful tool for differentiating your product or service—not just explaining why it is different, but explaining why the company *made* it different. Stop and think about that concept for a moment. Reflect on how much of an impact *why logic* can have with a prospect who is trying to tell the difference between your product or service and that of the competition.

As previously discussed, another significant reasoning point is your company's mission statement. How much more powerful would it be to explain *why* your company fostered a particular mission?

Using *why logic* you can explain *why* customers have such better outcomes using your product or service. Put yourself in their shoes! Isn't it important for the prospect to know not only that things will go better for them if they purchase your product or service, but also why your customers have better outcomes?

Again, one of the most important things that we must reason and resolve with a prospect is money. Money is the number one issue that must be resolved in a sales situation. If you can reason with the prospect as to why they should use their money to purchase your product or service, it will have a significant impact on the outcome of your presentation.

I think you can see that if you weave *why logic* through all aspects of the formula, you are more likely to reach the underlying motivations of your prospect and increase your conversions.

## RESOLVE

- settle or find a solution to a problem or matter

- deal with a question conclusively

- decide firmly on a course of action

- have the determination to do something

The final segment of our R3R1 formula is *resolve*. By this, I don't mean the salesperson must have the resolve to see things through to the finish. I mean, one must address any issues that the prospect may have. You want to accomplish the following:

- Settle or find a solution to a problem or matter
- Deal with a question conclusively
- Decide firmly on a course of action
- Have the determination to do something

Depending on the product, service, price point, competition, or any number of factors, there may be a lot of issues to resolve before hearing a yes from your prospect. Factors such as money, needs, selection/choice, deliverables, and many others need to be understood, addressed, and overcome if you expect to succeed. Let's go through some of these major issues that are found throughout a typical sales cycle, regardless of the industry, to get a better understanding of what to do, how to do it, and why you should do it.

# THREE ASPECTS OF MONEY

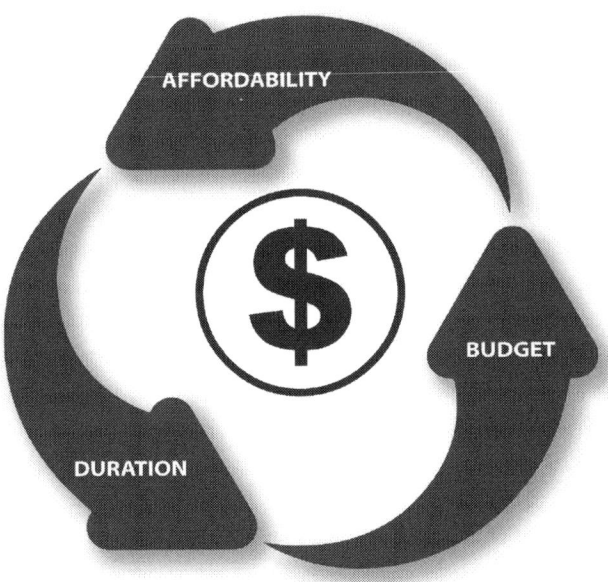

# *Money*

*Find the money, find the sale!*

"Money is no object." Isn't that what most of your prospects say when it comes to buying your product or service? Of course not! It's all about the money, and money is the silent objection that is killing sales. How is this objection silent? Most prospects will not openly discuss money issues with you. Conversely, most salespeople are not very good at talking about money with their prospects. Unfortunately, this is the case even though money is one of the most important issues that influences the decision to buy your product or service.

Are you routinely addressing money issues with prospects? Talking about money might make you uncomfortable or even nervous, but it is essential to being able to sell your product or service.

Individuals can most likely be grouped into one of the following categories:

1. They don't have the money.
2. They have the money but don't want to spend it.
3. They have the money and are willing to spend it.
4. Money is not an issue.

The silent objection is when the prospect can afford your product or service, but convinces themselves that they can't—and thus they never discuss the issue with you. Obviously, the group that needs the most attention is the group that has the money and doesn't want to spend it.

Consider an example from the senior housing industry. The approximate national average rent for an apartment in an independent retirement community is $2,400 per month, or $28,800 annually. Think about this for a moment. If the rent of an apartment in a retirement community were the same as (or less than) what a prospective resident would pay to live in their current home, how many empty apartments would there be in the retirement community? The answer, of course, is none. How many vacancies would you ever have? The same answer: none. Unfortunately, the reality is that many seniors cannot afford *not* to use the service. If the money issues have never been adequately addressed, they say that they are going to go "think over their options." But, as I mentioned earlier, *maybe* equals *no*, which applies here because they've already made the decision that it's too expensive. They have decided that they are going to stay with the status quo—the *do-nothing* decision.

Let's look at another example: that of an expensive new car. A well-qualified prospect visits a car dealership and looks at their most expensive model—a model he could certainly afford. However, because of his conservative values, he would never buy such an expensive car. Will he disclose what he is thinking to the salesperson? Or will he simply tell the salesperson that he is going home to think about his decision? While he stands there talking to the salesperson, he has already decided. The decision is to keep his old car, keep his money in the bank, and purchase a less expensive car.

Could a similar thing be happening to you when you are talking with your prospects? Regardless of what you are selling, you must have well-prepared reasoning and resolving statements to resolve your prospects money concerns. If not, you could be losing business.

What did the salesperson in that last situation do wrong? He assumed that anyone that could afford the expensive model would be excited enough by the product to buy it. That assumption is a major flaw.

The prospect that needs to be *sold* on the value of owning the car is not going to just purchase the vehicle. They are going to need to be reasoned with on issues relating to money, even if they have plenty. In the end, the problem of the car being extremely high-priced could be insurmountable. However, could the salesperson have switched the prospect to a slightly less expensive model and convinced him that he was getting a better value, yet still be the owner of a luxury vehicle? Yes, he could have. Maybe the issue with this prospect is that he does not believe in having debt, so the only way he would buy the car is with cash. Therefore, he is going to feel the pain of paying for the new car all at once. Did the salesperson uncover this information? By *relating, reasoning,* and *resolving,* the salesperson could have discovered these issues. We must be prepared to discuss affordability issues, budget, and beliefs.

How could this salesperson have improved his performance and made the sale?

First, when the salesperson starts to relate with the prospect, he determines that the candidate owns a successful business that he started on his own. He also finds out that he lives in an average-priced neighborhood. He asks the individual, "Would you like to buy or lease your next car?" The prospect tells him that he purchases all his cars because he does not like to have any debt. The salesperson tells the prospect that some customers who consider this model have trouble justifying the price of the car, especially if they are going to pay cash for it. The salesperson follows up with the question, "Does this sound like it might be like your situation?" The salesperson attempts to bring up the major obstacle—the fact that this conservative business owner will have to write a check for a car that is nearly half the price of his home! The prospect answers his question: "You know, I just do not think there is a scenario where I could ever justify spending that much money at one time on a car." Logically, this individual needs to be directed to a lower-priced car, as we discussed earlier.

How could the salesperson determine all of this without some probing? He couldn't! Let's say the question about money prompted this response: "If I were convinced that this vehicle would last a long time, I would probably spend the money. My company just got a big contract, and I have decided that I am going to get a nicer car and house." The salesperson could spend his time explaining the long-term value of the vehicle. Even with this type of response, if need be, he should still be prepared to down-sell the prospect to a less expensive car. Ultimately, if he does not address the money, he is dead from the beginning.

## *Duration*

Another issue to consider when discussing finances is that of duration. In other words, how long the prospect will have to pay for the product or how long they will need to use the service. Matters relating to the timeline need to be reviewed with every prospect.

A product or service may only be used for a specific amount of time. The cost of it may be paid in one payment, or in multiple payments over a period of time. So the prospect's question is, "How long am I going to need to pay for the product or service?"

It is important that you understand what the cost is for the duration of the standard time that your customers use the product or service and explain that information clearly to the prospect.

Duration is an easy thing to discuss. How long will the prospect have to pay for the product or service? How long will they use or need the product or service? It is essential that you know the statistics on the use of your product or service to have intelligent answers and discussions.

In many cases, a prospect is going to be in a situation where, once everything is weighed, the only logical financial decision is to make the purchase.

At times, it might be necessary to discuss alternatives if the prospect does not buy your product or service. What are they going to do in the future if they neglect their problem? The issues that caused them to inquire are not going away; most likely, they will continue to deteriorate.

## *Price/Cost Analysis*

Sometimes it makes sense to use a price/cost analysis so your prospect can understand that the price and the cost can be entirely different. For example, I got the idea that I wanted to own a high-performance vehicle some years ago, so I bought one. I paid cash for the car, $25,000, and it was several years old but had low miles. The first year I owned it, I paid around $4,000 in maintenance costs. The second year, I paid another $5,000 in maintenance costs. The third year, the mechanic told me the car needed repairs more than $12,000.

What is the point? The *price* for buying the car was only $25,000, but the *cost* of owning the car for three years was $46,000, which equaled a monthly payment of $1,277. By the way, I traded in the car for a new car with a maintenance warranty.

We must have a price/cost analysis for our particular product or service and help our prospects understand the difference between price and cost. The more you educate your prospect, the more likely they will reach the buy decision.

Money issues must be addressed head-on. You cannot wait for the prospect to draw conclusions about money without your guidance, since they can easily draw the wrong conclusion. You must lead this discussion, educate them, and steer them to the conclusion you want to see ... which is the sale being concluded. Leading the discussion on money is another great reasoning and resolving point. Using a variety of strategies, you can smoke out one of the most significant silent objections.

I can't repeat it enough: *Find the money, find the sale.*

# *Needs*

The idea of discussing the needs of the prospect seems straightforward. When I was an insurance agent trainee, the company I worked for showed the group a video from the 1950s called "Look for the Loss." It was an old, grainy black-and-white movie. It discussed how an agent could be successful by considering a prospect's situation and determining where their financial loss would occur, and then fill that loss with their product—life insurance. "Look for the Loss" was a powerful lesson that I never forgot, and I looked for the loss throughout the years that I sold life insurance. Good salespeople are very skillful at finding the needs of their prospects and then explaining how their product or service will solve that problem, the foundation of need-based selling.

However, I have discovered that salespeople are habitually in a hurry to dive into the needs too early in the discussion. In many cases, the timing is wrong because there is no relationship between the salesperson and the prospect, and therefore there is not any trust established.

The time to delve into the prospect's needs is when you have advanced to the resolving stage of the presentation. However, this is done *after* you have thoroughly related and reasoned with the prospect and after you've established a real basis for discussing their personal needs. When this discussion is initiated, you are going to work out solutions and resolve the obstacles that could keep this prospect from moving forward.

What if the prospect introduces their needs early in the discussion? Do you need to answer their questions at that time? Occasionally a prospect will bring up needs, but you will find that if you are in control of your sales presentation and wait to address their needs until the resolve portion, you will gain momentum toward closing the deal in a way you could not have done earlier in your presentation.

Think about this. Does it make sense to get into how you are going to solve someone's problems *before* you get to know them, *before* you find out why they are interested in your product or service, *before* you know what questions they have (which are usually not about costs and needs)?

The logical development of the presentation is as follows:

- Who is the company?
- Why is your product or service different?
- What is your mission?
- Why should they use your product or service?
- What is their financial situation?
- What are their specific needs?

Think about someone coming into a business and, after a very brief get-to-know-each-other session, the salesperson starts to ask questions about your needs. You are likely asking yourself, "Why should I trust you? Why should I trust your company? You are not my friend or adviser, so why should I talk to about my personal needs?" Apparently, the salesperson did not build a strong enough relationship with you.

Again, this is a situation when the prospect rejects the salesperson's recommendations and will usually not divulge the real reason; it is another silent sales killer. They will only tell you that they want to "think about it" when they have already rejected your recommendation. They may feel that it is impolite just to tell you what they think. They don't know you or your company and don't trust you. They lacked sufficient information to take the risk of doing business with you.

What's the hurry? What will you learn in the early part of your presentation that is going to change what you need to know? Instead, if you wait to learn about their needs later in the presentation, you are building trust and respect. No doubt at this point the prospect will respond better to your recommendations.

# *The Product*

The *deliverables* part of a presentation is the section most salespeople love. They enjoy showing their product or describing their service to prospects. Many salespeople believe this is when they are selling. The problem is, they're wrong. Ironically, this is the least important part of a presentation, but it is usually the part where most salespeople spend much of their time.

I was trained to show or explain the deliverables using the traditional *feature, advantage, benefit* presentation, also known as the FAB approach. It is not a bad tactic, but rather than just explaining things using the old FAB method, doesn't it make more sense also to explain the deliverables in a way that explains *why* the prospect will have a better outcome if he uses your product or service? Additionally, it makes sense to explain how your company's application of the product or service aligns with the prospect's goals.

> *Example: Beyond the FAB Approach*
>
> A salesperson is attempting to sell you a brand-new Harley-Davidson Heritage Softail Classic. He tells you that this motorcycle has the newest air-cooled, high-output Twin Cam 103B™, a 1753cc engine that produces ninety-three horsepower. He goes on to explain the advantages of the larger engine: It will get you out of the way of any obstacle on the road, and the counterbalancing feature gives a smooth ride with minimal vibration. He then says that new owners have

reported that they are enjoying the improvement of the larger counterbalanced engine because they can ride for hours comfortably through all kinds of terrain. Lastly, he explains that Harley has been able to retain the classic traditional designs for over one hundred years, which is in line with their mission—to deliver a traditional American motorcycle experience to their riders.

Take a moment and ask yourself: "Am I just *showing* my product or service, or am I *explaining* how they are going to have a better outcome using the product or service and that they are going to benefit by using it?" Also, "Am I weaving the company's mission through my presentation?"

You may have a desire to jump to showing the deliverables early in your presentation, but when you do that, you are stifling your presentation. Some prospects may want to try to force you to show them something early in the presentation. We have all experienced this situation. If your prospect gets squirmy and wants to look, then provide them with a small portion of the deliverables section of the presentation—then get back on your track and resume relating, reasoning, or resolving.

Remember, *showing* is not going to sell them, and relating, reasoning, and resolving are not showing.

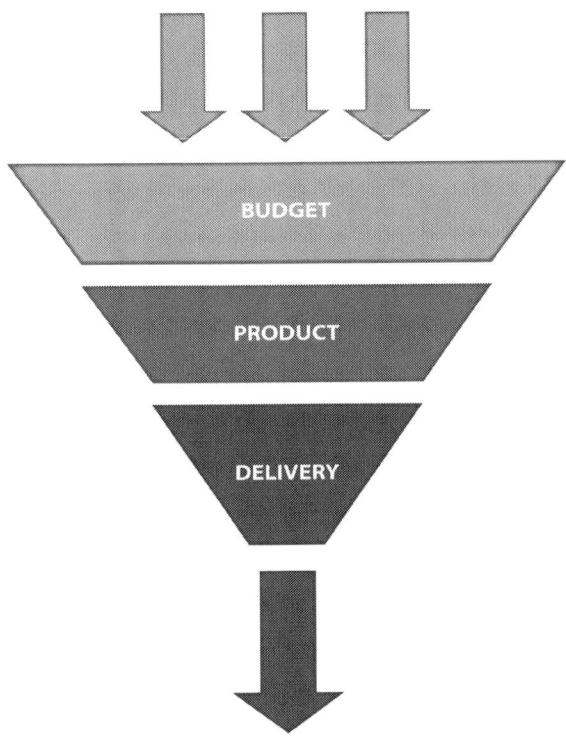

## *Selection*

Narrowing the selection down to a particular product or service isn't always that simple. One school of thought says you should delay this part of the resolving process until you are convinced that the prospect is more committed. However, until someone is fixed on a particular product or service, it is almost impossible to close the sale.

I hear a lot of people say "Don't most salespeople have an efficient narrow-down process?" The answer is simply, "No." This process is skipped in most sales presentations until the prospect initiates strong buying signals—which means that the salesperson is not leading the presentation.

Let's go over what you are trying to accomplish by using a narrow-down process in addition to relying on the prospect's selection of a product or service.

It is imperative that you have all the possible choices clearly spelled out in a document or other promotional materials so the prospect can *see* the options and isn't just listening as you describe the selections with words. Visuals are crucial in the narrow-down process. A simple visual list of options and features is essential. If you do not have promotional materials listing options and availability, create a document for your use. If you are selling different types of products or services, you may want to have a unique set of descriptions for each one. You can indicate if a product or service has limited availability or is sold out. The narrow-down process creates more demand for remaining products. It is imperative that you use the document during this portion of your presentation because it is very powerful when the prospect is looking at the paper and sees that only one product or service meets their criteria.

Let's use an example that fits this description: selling cruise travel. If you know anything about cruise travel, you know that there are endless options, from destinations to the number of nights to ships and, of course, to costs. There is a process involved to narrow down, using the proper questions, which will be the best cruise choice for that prospect. Using marketing materials that can show a client these options leads the conversation to a logical conclusion; they will decide which they like the most and will want to know everything about that option.

At this point, you have identified the product or service within the prospect's budget because you have already discussed financial issues, duration of need, and what they can afford to spend. Now you are *resolving* which products or services in your inventory appeal to the prospect and are going to address the issues that you (and the prospect) have identified, as well as falling in line with their budget.

Although I have shared the narrow-down process with dozens of salespeople, when I follow up later to see how the implementation of the process is going, I find that virtually none of them stick with the process. They are cheating themselves out of sales! Once you have found the one and only solution for the prospect, it is much easier to close the sale. In fact, if a prospect cannot select a particular product or service, it is almost impossible to close the deal.

Narrowing down is a simple step that is easy to neglect, but do not overlook the fact that people are very visual. We make decisions not only by what we hear, but by what we see. Using a narrow-down process that includes both spoken and written elements produces far better results.

## *Incentives*

When I was a young salesperson working with my brother, Rick, he would say to me, "Don't give your sales tools away." What he meant was, "Do not use your incentives too quickly or at the wrong time in your sales presentation."

As desperately as the accountants (and perhaps others) don't want you to use or offer incentives, they are a necessary part of business. They allow you to create demand for products and services as well as to motivate prospects to move forward.

Incentives must be used for one of three reasons:

1. To create demand for a product or service where there is no established market
2. To resolve various issues as they relate to deliverables
3. To get the prospect to move forward *now*

If properly used, incentives are highly effective at increasing sales, especially if they are used at the end of a well-crafted sales presentation. I am not referring to advertising promotional offers, which are efficient at moving unwanted inventory. I'm talking about those particular financial arrangements used during a sales opportunity that can improve the chances of closing the deal.

Again, what is the purpose of the incentive, and when should it be used? The purpose is to motivate the prospect to act *now*. You need to be resolving obstacles that are preventing the prospect from deciding by using available incentives. That is why incentives should be used at the end of the selection process—when you are asking for the order. You shouldn't be using incentives until the time is right! Otherwise, the incentive can lose its effectiveness, and you are only giving away a powerful tool for closing the sale. Incentives work, but if improperly used they can lose their effectiveness and become merely a cost of doing business. Incentives are more effective when combined with moral suasion, reasoning, and education of prospects (which I will speak to in a few moments).

When an incentive is used, you must have justification as to why you can offer it. The use of incentives is mutually beneficial for both parties.

Here is an example of the use of an incentive and how a company explains why they are willing to offer the incentive, and how it is mutually beneficial to the customer and the company.

> *Incentive Example: Replacement Windows*
>
> A home improvement company is installing replacement windows in a house in a certain neighborhood, so they will go to *all* the houses on the street and let them all know that if they order windows, they'll get a 10 percent discount *if* they can take delivery during the same week as their neighbor. The reason? The installation crew will already be there, so the cost is slightly lower to the company, and the company is willing to pass along those savings to you!

Can you see how the explanation of both the *what* and *why* of the incentive is so powerful?

If you do not explain why you can offer the prospect an incentive and why your company is benefiting from them doing the transaction now, it can seem like the incentive is a made-up arrangement, and the prospect may lose confidence in your offering. It is imperative that you clearly explain why you can offer the incentive.

## *Moral Suasion, Reasoning, and Education*

To motivate prospects, it is not only important to use properly crafted incentives, but you must also combine them with moral suasion, reasoning, and education.

> *Moral Suasion: Using a moral argument to persuade the prospect that the only right thing to do is to utilize your product or service.*

In certain businesses, such as life insurance, a salesperson can develop moral suasion arguments. An example of moral suasion would be a business owner purchasing a key-man insurance policy on himself to ensure that his company can continue and employees can maintain employment, and perhaps buy his family out of the business if he dies prematurely.

If there is not a moral basis to construct a presentation, then reasoning with the prospect about why they will be better off using your product or service is the only logical course of action. That is another presentation that can and should be made.

Educating or providing an explanation using the statistical reasons why your customers are better off than people who decide not to use your product or service is also very effective.

If moral suasion, reasoning, and educating can be combined with a well-placed and justified incentive, you will have a compelling presentation that will motivate many prospects to move forward now.

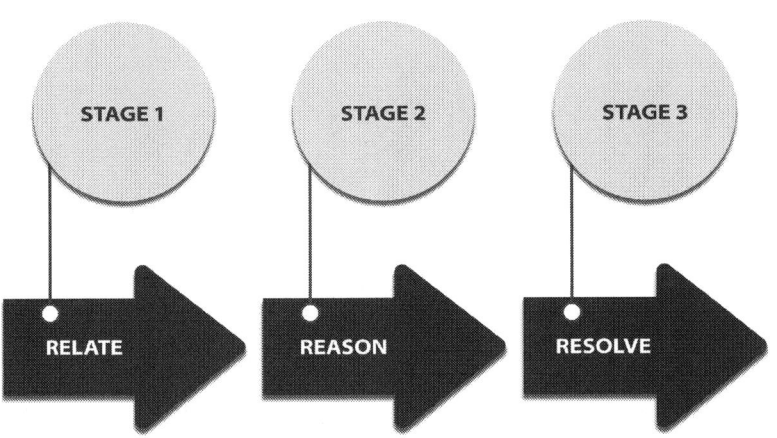

## *The Close*

Most salespeople love to discuss closing techniques. They like to talk about the close that convinced the person to say yes. These stories are like fish tales—they are often embellished. "There I was—the biggest contract the company had ever seen—and they were walking out the door when I said …" You get the idea.

Their big story centers on when the prospect was asked to buy using a certain line of reasoning, they said yes, and, as a direct result, the sale was closed. However, I allege that the actual closing section of a presentation is one of the least important parts, next to showing the deliverables. Here is why I am making that assertion. You must be closing the sale from the time you say "Hello, my name is," and during every stage from that moment forward. If you are waiting to commit your prospect to purchase your product or service until the end of your presentation by using some smooth lines, you are going to be sorely disappointed. If you have done your job of closing from the beginning, you will reach the right conclusion.

Even though you are closing from the beginning, this does not mean that you do not have to ask the prospect to buy. You *must* ask the prospect to buy your product or service. Most prospects do not buy on their own. A significant number of sales are not consummated simply because the salesperson did not directly ask the prospect to buy. Be direct! As already mentioned, you should know if your prospect is buying way before the point you ask them to write a check.

Let's review a few significant points. You should have a strong indication if your prospect is buying during the part of the presentation where you are sitting down and relating. You should be asking yourself during the relating section of the presentation, "How is this meeting going?" If it is not going well at that stage, they are not buying from you. No fabulous closing line is going to turn this ship around. They do not like you, and this sale is not going anywhere. Let's assume that the relating is going well—you find out their questions, and they are all buying questions, like "How much does it cost?" or "What is your availability?" You proceed to the next step and uncover why they are looking at your product or service. You find out that they have a particular problem. They tell you what the problem is, and you commit them to the fact that your product or service is going to solve their problem—that went well. Next, you explain what your company is, what its mission is, why the prospect should use your company's service, and why they will fare better. The prospect demonstrates through comments and body language that they like what they hear. The next part is another big part of closing the sale. You asked a series of commitment questions, and based on the answer to those questions you have more indications of the prospect's willingness to commit.

You begin resolving obstacles related to which product or service they want, need, and can afford. You show the deliverables and explain why they solve the problems that were uncovered. Then you do the narrow-down or select the particular product or service. At that point, the prospect says, "Yes, this is the one." Finally, you ask the prospect to buy. Sure, that is what people call "the close." But, based on the previous steps, when did the close begin? At "Hello," of course!

When you ask the prospect to buy, you need to explain what they need to do to purchase the product or service. The process of asking the prospect for the business should be assumptive—it is not closing, but only asking to buy. Everyone whom you meet and subsequently engage in a presentation, regardless of how well the presentation goes, needs to receive *The Ask*. When you have perfected your sales process, you will know based on the progression of the presentation if the prospect is likely going to buy.

The reason everyone needs to ask is as follows:

> *People are sophisticated, complicated, and the total of their life experiences.*

Remember this phrase, and you will have greater success! As good as any of us *think* we are at reading prospects, you can never actually understand all of them. Never assume they are not buying as they are going along with your presentation, because they might be. Perhaps they are not expressive. With this type of prospect, if you don't ask them to buy, unfortunately, they will just leave without buying, which is a common mistake of salespeople. So, when building or improving your sales presentation, make sure to include a section that explains to each prospect how to buy your product or service.

Perhaps it is the prospect's first visit to your place of business. Do not assume they will not make an immediate decision. Some salespeople believe that a candidate cannot make a buying decision the first time they meet them, and this simply isn't the case. If you have been able to complete your presentation and they have all the facts required to make a decision, they can make it now. Some prospects may want to consider things for a few hours or a day. In the next chapter, we will discuss how to commit that prospect. When the prospect goes to the "think it over" phase, that is a real test of your sales presentation. Have you done a thorough job of relating, reasoning, and resolving?

If you have done an excellent job of giving your presentation, you should close a significant number of your sales within a short time of making the presentation. If the prospect does not commit within a brief timeframe, they are usually cooling off.

## *Time to Decide*

It is important to plan for the reality that a certain number of prospects are unwilling to decide at the first meeting and will ask for time to weigh their decision. However, if they have gone through the narrow-down process and have selected a particular product or service, that is a commitment of sorts. If you cannot conclude the sale right then, you should set a specific appointment for a follow-up discussion and decision. You need to get a commitment on a date and time where your prospect *can* decide.

You should not end the meeting without making another appointment. If the candidate will not commit to a specific appointment, that is a bad sign. The prospect is, in effect, telling you no. On the other hand, if they commit to a follow-up meeting, then you want to quickly review what was established during your presentation, including the product or service they have selected.

You could say something like this: "Well, let's do this while you are thinking it over. I will hold the product or service you selected for twenty-four hours (or another deadline). I am also going to write you a receipt (or proposal, or contract) to recall our discussion."

Then you write on the receipt the deal points, including any incentives you have promised. Date and sign the receipt, making it an official agreement. The receipt or contract is what they will use if they proceed. You are not asking them to sign it; you just sign it.

Think of this from the prospect's perspective. The prospect has all the deal points spelled out on an official document, and all they should do is write a check or call with a credit card. Like many other pieces of the puzzle, this was something I discovered by doing it just once. It must become part of your process. You do not want prospects walking away without either making a commitment, writing a check, or being on a twenty-four-hour close with a receipt or contract in their hand. The use of a written agreement or receipting works in this situation. I have written hundreds of receipts on twenty-four closes, and it is highly effective.

## *Gifting, Reassurance, and Cancellations*

Have you ever overlooked the opportunity to reassure a prospect that is making a commitment? Reassuring is another crucial step in the sales presentation and should not be neglected. If the prospect has made a commitment and written a check or is on the twenty-four-hour close with a contract or receipt in hand, you must give them a small gift and reassure them that their decision is the right one.

*Gifting*

Let's take a few minutes and discuss offering gifts to your prospects. The thought behind making sure that you always have a small gift to give a prospect who inquires about your product or service is based on the theory of reciprocation. Reciprocation means that if someone does something for us, then we are more likely to want to do something for them. For example, if you and your spouse are invited to a friend's home for dinner, you are more likely also to extend an invitation to your house for dinner. In fact, you may even feel obligated.

In a popular sitcom, the main character never wants certain acquaintances to do anything for him because he does not want to feel obligated to do anything for them. We laugh as we watch him work extremely hard to avoid getting into this situation. Your prospect can behave similarly. Some people will try to turn down your gift, especially those who are leaving to "think over" your proposal. They are telling you no, and they do not want to feel obligated to you or your business proposal.

*Reassurance*

Reassurance is especially necessary when someone meets with you for the first time, and because of your fantastic presentation they make the decision to move forward. If you allow the prospect to leave without spending a few minutes discussing why the decision is right, why they are going to come out better, and how they are going to love your product or service, your buyer can go away and develop buyer's remorse. You know what I am talking about—all of us have had buyer's remorse at one time or another. Buyer's remorse can happen to your prospect even if you reassure them after they make the decision. Your prospect calls you back a day later or a week later and cancels, giving you an irrational reason for not wanting to move forward, and you just cannot talk them back into it. You have lost the sale.

They left and decided to do nothing, to remain status quo. Remember, it is easy to do nothing because you don't have to do anything to do nothing. To not decide *is* to decide. It is to choose to do nothing.

*Cancellations*

If you never have a prospect cancel on you, then you need to ask yourself, "Am I selling, or am I only having people buy from me?" There is a big difference. If you are truly selling, you are going to have cancellations. Why? When you are selling, you are relating, reasoning, and resolving. You are engulfing the prospect with reasons and resolving the issues that are keeping them from moving forward. Therefore, some of the people you sell are going to back out even if you reassure them.

That's not to say, of course, that you can't get some of these prospects back on board! You simply need to have a process in place to walk through the eventualities that will lead to a final decision. What should you do when a prospect calls to cancel because they have buyer's remorse?

*Example: Cancellation Dialogue*

Salesperson: "What you are telling me is no, you are not going to buy my product or service like we discussed yesterday, is that correct?" (You need to see how committed to this new decision they are.)

Prospect: "That is right. I have decided that I am not going to move forward now."

Salesperson: "I accept your answer. However, I do not believe you are making the right decision, and I believe you should reconsider." (You want them to know you are accepting what they are telling you so they are not defensive, but you should then say clearly that you do not agree with what they are doing.)

Salesperson: "I believe you should move forward for all of the reasons we agreed to yesterday. What has changed since yesterday?" (Then wait for them to tell you.)

If you conclude that they are fearful and could be re-convinced, make an appointment to meet with them and discuss it again. If you believe they have dug in their heels and are committed to staying status quo, then move on.

I want to reiterate that if cancellations are not happening to you on a regular basis, you are not working hard enough to persuade your prospects to buy your product and service through the relating, reasoning, and resolving process.

# R3R1 SALES PROCESS

# R3R1 SALES PROCESS

The systematic sales method involving a sequence of steps to assist sales professionals in increasing closing ratios.

Sales strategy, sales presentation, sales track—whatever name you prefer, this is a step-by-step plan during your sales process to lead to the desired result, the sale. Every company needs a solid sales presentation. The presentation allows the salesperson to know where they are on the track and ultimately how the presentation is coming along.

Many people say that they cannot use a set or "canned" sales presentation. That belief is like a stage actor not having any lines. The best actors make you believe they are the character they are portraying. A professional actor's role is much harder than using a set presentation. When I deliver a sales presentation, I am portraying myself. I am who I am. I am not faking anything—I am just giving a logical presentation that covers the information that I know is needed for the prospect to come to the decided conclusion. I want the prospect to believe me. I want them to trust my company. I want them to understand my company's mission. I want them to know I understand their needs. I want them to know why my product is different from everyone else's product. I want them to know why they are going to be better off if they use my product. I want them to know I understand their money concerns. I want them to understand that I can work out the deliverables.

I have been in business for many years, and I do not know how salespeople can wing a presentation and not end up with terrible results. *R3R1: The Sales Formula for Success* and the sales track discussed in this book is an example of an organized sales presentation.

As you review the R3R1 sales process, you may be thinking that there are a lot of steps in the process. I agree! People want to oversimplify selling, but the truth is that the sales process is not simple, and if you are just winging it, you will see that in your results. Typically, it is somewhat of a complicated process to sell an expensive product. In general, most sales professionals are not selling low-cost products. It's not a complicated process to sell a box of pens to one person, but it may be incredibly complex to sell 500,000 boxes of pens to one company. So logically, there will be several steps throughout the sales process to persuade someone to make a significant purchase.

One thing to keep in mind is that even though there are multiple steps in the process, they are not all being performed in the same amount of time. For example, in a speed messaging situation, you should be able to deliver your key *reasoning* points in less than two minutes if necessary. So, various aspects of the sales process may be quicker at times or more time-consuming based on what is required. In some sales situations, the entire sales process can be accomplished in thirty minutes. In other circumstances, it might be three hours and yet others might require several meetings over some weeks.

Again, closely consider the R3R1 sales process and ask yourself which one of the steps in the process you could omit without affecting the outcome of some of your presentations. Could you skip the warm-up and go directly to qualifying the prospect?

You could dispatch with finding out why the prospect inquired about your product. Many salespeople skip the entire reasoning section of their sales process, which includes a suitability presentation. Skip telling the prospect anything about your company. Don't take the time to explain why your product is different. Why bother telling the prospect about your company's mission and how it aligns with their goals? Lastly, you could omit to mention that your customers have far better outcomes using your product.

Do you see where I am going? You can skip these steps of the sales process, but you may be missing out on selling many prospects who would have otherwise bought your product if you had simply covered this information.

Since this is not easy, it is important to have an outline of your sales process and review it frequently. If you don't have an outline, you may forget steps and omit them from your presentation, which will reduce your sales efficiency. We are instant forgetters and tend to wander off task, so don't get caught in that trap!

Why do pilots review a checklist before every flight? Don't they just memorize everything? No way! Imagine forgetting one little thing that happens to be critical. Do you want to be on that flight? Their lives and the lives of their passengers depend on them staying on task. A written sales process, like the example at the end of this section, is the same. If you do not have one and do not review it daily, you will start to wander and shortcut aspects of the process, and it will affect your closing percentages.

The review is something I have practiced for many years. Every day, before any interactions with a prospect, I review my sales process and think about the steps and whether I've been skipping any key portions of my presentation. Additionally, if I used some new sub-process successfully, I will write it in and begin to add it to my standard presentation. If I don't do this, how will I know what works and what doesn't? How will I ever improve? Remember, knowing and doing are two different things. I may *know* how to do something, but I may not be executing correctly. In sales, everything is about execution, so I need to keep myself sharp—and this is one of the strongest techniques to use. We know that some salespeople are either new to the sales business or may have never received adequate training on what selling is. If they write out their sales process list and review it, will they necessarily improve? No, because they are not using an effective process. However, R3R1 works! As stated before, although there are multiple steps in the entire process, they can be summarized in the three main sections:

1. Did I relate?
2. Did I reason?
3. Did I resolve?

The R3R1 process contains all the fundamental steps of the *relate, reason, resolve* method. Of course, salespeople need to take what they learn and make it their own, so you can modify R3R1 to build your own plan that contains steps that are unique to your product and sales presentation. However, the three Rs remain the key to obtaining that final, all-important R.

## *Using All Three Rs*

Once you have determined that you are dealing with a legitimate prospect, one who can decide one way or the other, then it is imperative that your presentation of relating, reasoning, and resolving be so impressive that it just *overwhelms* the prospect. Yes, overwhelms them. Overwhelming means that the prospect believes that the only logical thing to do is to tell you yes. How do you like that idea? Yes is the goal, after all. Your presentation must be tight. It must be compelling, and *you* must be compelling. Your presentation needs to be passionate and meaningful every time you give it.

Again, I want you to think about the idea of overwhelming the prospect with your presentation—in a good way. You need to be a breath of fresh air, befriending them, informing them, and helping them work out the issues that stand in the way of their moving forward with your product or service.

If the idea of overwhelming a prospect is offensive to you in any way, I apologize, but at the same time, I don't. You see, this is an excellent sales concept, and you should keep an open mind. After all, the culmination of a good sales presentation is to compel the prospect to move forward *now*.

# R3R1 Sales Process

## Relate

Warm-up
Initial Qualifying
The Why
Questions and Answers
Defensive Qualifying

## Reason

Company Presentation
Differentiation Statements
Mission Statement Presentation
Mission Statement Commitment
Review Outcomes and Experience
Suitability Presentation

## Resolve

Money
Needs
Selection
Deliverables
The Ask
Reassurance
Gifting

## RESULTS

- desirable or beneficial consequences, outcomes, or effects

- having obtained a notable or successful response; to have been effective

Now we proceed to the exciting part of sales, the results! Well, it's exciting if you're doing things right and closing business. With the R3R1 formula, I know from experience that you will like your results!

Once you understand the fundamentals of relating, reasoning, and resolving (R3), you will achieve the results (R1) you want. R3 holds the key to unlocking your sales presentations, and you will now close a greater number of those sales. R1 means that you are going to increase earned commissions, since you are learning the sales process that leads to efficiency.

The exciting thing is that you will be doing the same job but making more money! Perhaps you were delivering ten sales presentations a week and closing two. You begin using the R3R1 process, you close four—think about your long-term outlook! The adversity you have previously experienced when it's hard to achieve sales results will be reduced since you now have a clear path. Where you have been and where you are going will be as different as night and day. Now you are equipped with the knowledge needed to be a top performer. Your company will be happier because of your new success and the positive impact on the business.

I cannot express to you the feelings of satisfaction you will have by exceeding your sales objectives. Once you have gained this knowledge, keep learning and keep perfecting your use of R3, and you will reach the highest level of results.

# THE R3R1 RECAP

Now that we've spent plenty of time digging into what makes up the R3R1 formula, let's recap everything. As you review these definitions for *relate*, *reason*, *resolve*, and *results*, think about how you will implement this formula in your sales process.

## Step 1: Relate

- make a connection
- have or establish a relationship
- interact
- respond, especially favorably

When it comes to relating, are you developing relationships with your prospects to get them to respond positively? Are you strengthening the relationships by finding out things about your potential customer as well as sharing things about yourself?

## Step 2: Reason

- think through logically
- conclude or infer
- convince, persuade by reasoning
- an explanation of a situation or circumstance which made certain results seem possible or appropriate

As you consider this stage of the presentation, are you making compelling arguments to prospects using the *foundations of reasoning* to persuade the prospect to see things your way and conclude that the only logical decision is for them to purchase your product?

## Step 3: Resolve

- settle or find a solution to a problem or matter
- deal with a question conclusively

- decide firmly on a course of action
- the determination to do something

Are you able to resolve problems and obstacles for your prospects that are keeping them from moving forward so that they can make a firm decision to proceed?

## *Step 4: Results*

- a desirable or beneficial consequence, outcome, or effect
- to obtain a notable or successful response; be effective

Selling your product or service to your prospect is the best outcome for everyone. The result you want for your prospect is to have a positive experience using your product. The result you want is to make more money.

Salespeople naturally vary in skills. Some may be good at relating, and others at resolving. However, very few salespeople are good at reasoning, and even fewer are skilled in the art of all three aspects of selling: relating, reasoning, and resolving. When you master all three skills, you can take your professional growth to a higher level and accomplish things that will surprise even yourself!

## INSIGHTS

⇒ additional sales concepts to increase knowledge as it relates to the R3R1 sales process

If you stop reading this book now, you will already have a complete review of the R3R1 sales process. However, the next several chapters contain additional information that will help you become even more successful when implementing the process.

Over the years, I have worked with many great sales professionals and have gained lots of experience in the sales profession. Additionally, I have learned many techniques through my hard work. Here I will share many of the insights that I have discovered over the years in multiple industries that can easily be applied to your current situation.

In these chapters, I share a few additional concepts that will make you more successful in your application of the R3R1 sales process, and sales in general, so you can achieve maximum results.

Growing up on a farm in the Midwest, I always had a pragmatic approach to solving problems. I naturally wanted to understand why certain processes were performed in a certain way or if there could be another method to accomplish a task that would increase efficiency and results. I have used this analytical approach in honing my sales skills and have seen the effect of applying this knowledge to increase my closing percentages. Coming up are many of those concepts, which I'm sure you will find informative, creative, interesting, and beneficial to your current and future sales endeavors.

## *The Post-Mortem*

It is important that you review your presentations before you meet with a prospect—every single time. However, equally as important is to take your written sales track and review every presentation that you performed that day. Ask yourself if you covered all the steps of the presentation. "Did I skip steps? Did things go well (or poorly) during the performance?"

Think about your favorite sport. Do you think they aren't reviewing film of the game to look for ways to improve? Of course they are ... and if you're not doing this, don't you think you should? Make no mistake; it's difficult to conduct post-mortem sales presentation evaluations, which is why few people do them. The best sales professionals perform post-mortems on all their presentations. That is why they are the best salespeople! They allow themselves to make mistakes, recognize their mistakes, correct them, and improve their presentations. I conduct post-mortems after every sales presentation—win or lose—because there's always something that could be done differently to improve the overall performance.

You don't need to fixate on the particular presentation and the minor details; just identify areas you can improve during the next opportunity. Otherwise, your mental energy will be drained. After finishing the review of a loss, just put this word into your vocabulary: "Next!" The last presentation is over. You have analyzed it and have improved your skills for your next opportunity, or you closed a sale and earned a commission! Win or lose, you are moving forward.

# THE RELATING AND REASONING EFFECT

## BUYING

| Prospect Buying | Relating Decreases | Reasoning Decreases | Resolving Increases |

## NOT BUYING

| Prospect Not Buying | Relating Increases | Reasoning Increases | Resolving Decreases |

## Bought or Sold

To increase sales, it is imperative that you understand the *bought or sold* concept and what effect it has on your sales process and business in general. Some products are bought (watermelons); other products are mostly sold (life insurance). The fact that some products are bought and some are sold is important for business owners, managers, and salespeople to understand. The reality is that most products are bought *and* sold. Unfortunately, this causes complacency and warps planning efforts and motivation on selling the prospects who need to be sold.

Specifically, in the case where the product is being bought, you likely spend most of the time in the sales process resolving various issues, such as product selection and cost issues. You have a prospect who wants to buy the product, so reasoning goes to the wayside, and in many cases relating is at a minimum. So, you become conditioned to resolve—not to reason or relate. The problem is that a certain percentage of the prospects that you encounter will need to be sold! If you are conditioned to the buying customer, you are not putting forth the necessary effort toward the prospect that needs to be sold. This group may never buy your product or will buy from a competitor.

Let's look at some of the products that I have sold over the years. Although this is not scientific, it is my opinion of what percentages of these products were bought versus sold.

| Product or Service | Bought | Sold |
|---|---|---|
| • Watermelons | 100% | |
| • Replacement Siding and Windows | 10% | 90% |
| • Electrolux Vacuum Cleaners (door-to-door) | 5% | 95% |
| • Automobiles | 60% | 40% |
| • Life Insurance (If someone calls and wants to buy life insurance, the agent wonders if they are going to have someone done in!) | 5% | 95% |
| • B2B Application Software | | 100% |
| • Senior Housing (Average annual cost ranges between $24,000 and $48,000, with lifetime expenses at $72,000 to $144,000 and more.) | 20% | 80% |

Although I haven't personally been involved with the following products, my conclusions make logical sense when you apply the bought/sold concept.

- Apple Products      100% Bought

Why? When I go to this store, I do not have to be persuaded to purchase the latest, greatest product. I am there to make a purchase, and the staff can ring up the sale!

- Vacation Timeshares      100% Sold

I have sat through this type of presentation one time—and I was not sold.

It is critical to determine what percentage of your prospects will buy and what percentage will need to be sold. The higher the percentage of buyers, the more complacent your sales efforts will become. The lower the number of buyers and the more that need to be sold, the more focused the sales efforts must be. If you determine that you spend the majority of the sales opportunity resolving, then there is a lot of room for improvement.

## READINESS

**AS BUYING INCREASES SALES READINESS DECREASES**

*This chart is a hypothetical example and not based on the results of specific research.*

# *Demand*

How do you create demand for your product or service? Sell it! Unless people are buying your product or service, there is no demand, and therefore there is no value. The real value is always driven by demand for a product or service. Of utmost importance is the fact is that a product can be sold, and therefore, demand can be created for the product. You are in the *demand-creating* business. Stay focused on this fact, and work diligently to build demand for your product or service.

At times, salespeople may believe that demand already exists for their product or service. They become lackadaisical about their efforts, if the consumer is just simply going to buy their service because they want it. Most companies that have products with high consumer demand do not have highly paid salespeople employed to sell these products; the salespeople are simply order-takers. However, most businesses need salespeople who realize that they are the creators of demand.

In my career, I have only sold one product that had real demand. It was 1983, and I was selling Porsches, and it was the same year that the 944 Porsche was released. It was truly a revolutionary car. I saw one the other day, and it still looked good! When it came out, we had people coming into our showroom wanting to buy the car. The dealer I worked for also sold Volkswagens and Audis at that location, and at the time Audi was a relatively new vehicle in the United States. However, the 944 buyer was interested in the car because of its front engine design and innovative styling. The owner of the dealership had decided that he was not going to gouge his customers by asking for more than the sticker price. Here were the general terms of the deal:

1. The prospect could order whatever they wanted, and they would pay sticker price.
2. They would have to put a $5,000 deposit down.
3. They had to take immediate delivery when the car arrived.
4. If they wanted to order a non-standard color, they would have to pay in advance for the car.
5. If they had a trade-in, they would need to dispose of their vehicle themselves through whatever means they had. (The dealer did not want to get caught up in paying a customer more for their car to make a trade. It was unnecessary, because he had real demand for this car.)

The dealership was only allotted around fifty vehicles, and they were all sold. That is an example of actual demand. I have never sold another product or service since with real demand. All the other products needed significant selling, and there was some, little, or no demand for my product.

Even if there is robust demand for a product or service, it can wane in time. For example, look at Coca-Cola. There was a time when they could not produce Coca-Cola fast enough. However, today people are drinking significantly less soda, and the demand for Coca-Cola has declined.

The following example illustrated when I sold a product with no demand, the opposite of the Porsche story:

I was involved in the rollout of a software-as-a-service product, and the potential customers were college and university charitable foundations, community foundations, and other charitable organizations. This product had never existed before, and the charities did not even know why they needed it. A new software product is a classic example of selling a product with no demand and creating demand in a brand-new market. It is a long and challenging process to get customers to be early adopters of such a service.

Most products and services are somewhere in the middle, but understanding the fact that you are responsible for creating demand cannot be understated. If you believe that there is natural demand for your product or service, and you stop *reasoning* with prospects as to why they need to buy, you've made a terrible mistake.

**DON'T WASTE YOUR RESOURCES.**

**YOUR RESOURCES ARE TIME AND ENERGY.**

**YOUR TIME AND ENERGY ARE YOUR MONEY.**

**SPEND YOUR "MONEY" WISELY.**

# *Keeping Score*

I have only played golf a few times in my life so far. When I play golf, I always seem to do well. Do you know why? It's because I have never kept score! If I ever kept score, I would have to face the fact that I am a terrible golfer. Some salespeople operate under the same arrangement. They do not keep score. Thus, they are great salespeople.

However, in sales, there are few things more important than keeping score. You've likely heard the phrase "sales is a numbers game," but that is not the reason you need to keep close track of your score.

Here is what I mean by keeping score: Know your closing ratio. Now, when I discuss closing ratio, I am talking about when you give your *full* presentation to a *qualified* prospect. I'm certainly not speaking of those times when you have a brief conversation or leave a speed message for someone who never responds. I'm talking about those significant sales events when you run through your entire process. Your sales manager may be interested in knowing your closing ratio, but you should not need to be reminded to keep track of this statistic. You should always be aware of your closing ratio.

*Example: Closing Ratio*

Last week you gave five presentations to qualified prospects, which resulted in two closed sales. Simple math says your closing rate is 40 percent. But what is your closing rate goal? It's 100 percent! So, although 40 percent sounds nice, you failed 60 percent of the time, so you need to improve. Until you're giving five presentations and closing five sales, you're going to be working on improving your closing ratio. You want to be sure you're tracking this ratio carefully.

You may be thinking that this is very basic. However, I will tell you that I have worked with many salespeople who, when asked, could not tell me their closing ratio. These ratios need to be analyzed weekly, monthly, and even annually. This is the most important measurement you can have in sales! It tells you how well you are doing and where you might need to improve. If you are closing at a very high ratio and the numbers start to go down for some reason, maybe you are skipping key aspects of your sales process and need to review it to make sure you get back on track. Perhaps you need to look over your post-mortems, if you ascertain that you are not regularly performing the post-mortem review. Or maybe you are giving presentations to non-prospects. Again, this is for you to determine, but it cannot be done if you are not keeping score.

There is only one real score that counts, and it is your closing ratio. You must keep your numbers and know your score at all times. You must practice your game until your score is perfect. Until that time, you have room to improve.

## *Execution*

Typically, a manager wants her team to do a certain number of presentations per week. Depending on the product or service, the number could vary from one or two per week (in high-end sales) to five per week—as many as forty presentations for less complex products or services. A manager may determine that a salesperson is not meeting the matrix on the number of expected sales presentations per week. The manager may decide that the salesperson needs to increase his marketing efforts or may require more advertising support, or both.

The fact is that there are only so many presentations that can be done in a week. If your company requires that you make ten presentations a week and you are incredibly active and could arrange and perform twenty per week, could you increase that number to thirty or forty a week? No, not reasonably. It's simply a resource issue. Your primary resource is time, and you only have a certain amount available.

Sports are similar to sales. Take, for example, a professional football game. If you watch an average televised football game, how much time is spent by players running plays? Well, the average game takes about 174 minutes to televise, or just less than three hours to watch. So, the answer to the question is a whopping eleven minutes. That is 6 percent of the total game time. The other 94 percent of the time is spent watching players stand around, replays, analysis, coaches, cheerleaders, crowd, and commercials.

What does this have to do with selling? Everything. Owners and sales managers of companies can think that the salesperson just needs to deliver more presentations (or run more plays). The reality is that what needs to happen is you need to execute your presentations, your plays, better.

A football coach knows exactly how many plays he has left in a specific game, from beginning to end. He knows right where he is during the entire game. Does he think that he can get his players to run double the plays that they run in an average game? No. Even if he has the greater time of possession during the game, he knows the other side is going to have the ball as well. So what can he do to put more points on the board? Improve execution. Improve the performance of his players when they have possession of the ball.

Back to the sales manager: Where should the emphasis be? On how many sales presentations you make, or on the quality of the presentation?

If you put the emphasis on the increasing the number of presentations and not on execution, that would be the same as a football coach having his star running back run every play and never resting him. If the running back is a good player and plays with passion, he will simply wear himself out and underperform. That is why you will almost always see a coach pull a runner out after he completes a big run, to let him rest for a few minutes.

Of course, you need to do a certain number of presentations. However, if you are only concerned with increasing the number of presentations and not on the quality, you can lose your effectiveness and focus.

For example, my average sales presentation contains approximately seventeen steps and averages two hours and thirty minutes. I have found that if I deliver more than two presentations a day, I begin to lose my precision. I slip in my efficiency. I start to hear myself speaking. I also know that I am better if I have some time to rest between the first and the second presentations of the day. If they are back-to-back, I am not as sharp. Keep in mind, that is five hours of presentations a day. Also, my closing ratio on a third presentation goes down. We all have limits to our peak performance. Sometimes it's better to do fewer presentations and close more.

Another comparison is that of running a marathon slower rather than faster. The longer you run, the more wear and tear there is on your body. For example, if an average, well-trained athlete ran a marathon, he should be able to run it in three and a half hours, or 210 minutes of non-stop running. The world record holder in marathon running is Dennis Kimmeto. On September 28, 2014, Kimmeto set a new world record of 2:02:57 at the Berlin Marathon. He ran nonstop for 122 minutes and fifty-seven seconds, almost eighty-eight minutes less than an average, well-trained runner. If you can close 50 to 60 percent of your sales versus 20 to 30 percent, you do not have to perform as long to reach the same result, right? By making himself more efficient, Kimmeto cut the amount of work that he had to do by 42 percent. He attained the goal by running 42 percent less time than an average runner.

Performance is not about doing something longer; it is about doing it more efficiently. In sales, this is particularly the case. You may be saying that Kimmeto has natural abilities that enable him to reach higher levels of performance, and of course you'd be correct. Natural abilities in sales only account for part of your efficiency. Improvement comes from hard work and refining your sales process.

## *Strike While the Iron is Hot!*

An individual contacts your business and expresses a sincere interest in your product or service, and you determine that you are dealing with a qualified prospect. You are off to the races, and this race is going to be quick!

You must be mentally ready, once you have identified a qualified prospect interested in your product or service, to engage in the relating, reasoning, and resolving presentation. You need to be prepared to deliver the presentation as if you will never have another chance—because you probably won't.

The worst scenario is to let the prospect cool off, and the result is they decide to do nothing. All the momentum in the world is in the do-nothing category, and it is so easy to do nothing. Think about it. What is easier for you—to do something or nothing? It seems ridiculous, but it is a simple fact. It is always simpler to do nothing.

Sure, we have all had the person we have called on for two years and met with twenty-seven times, but that will not keep you in business. It is imperative that you strike when the prospect has a high level of interest. You need to be prepared *at that moment* to reason with the prospect and compel them to move forward now. Yes, your focus is on getting the prospect to make the commitment today. Any delay in decision-making is usually a lost sale. You must never forget to strike while the iron is hot.

## *Changing Lose to Win*

When I was a young salesperson, a concept was shared with me, and it helped me deal with adversity during my early years in sales. It's a concept called "Lose to Win." It's based on the premise that an outstanding professional baseball player may have a batting average of .300. Clearly, that means that the player does not get on base 70 percent of the time, so he is losing more than he is winning—yet he is a winner. Ty Cobb holds the Major League Baseball record for highest career batting average of .366.

The lesson is that it is okay for a salesperson not to sell the majority of their prospects because even if they don't, they are winning. This concept also promotes the belief that it is all right to feel the adversity of losing because they are still winners. "Lose to win" maintains that the adversity the salesperson feels by losing more than winning makes them stronger and more focused—much like a boxer feels when he gets the first hard punch in the face during a prize fight, or when a quarterback gets sacked for the first time during a playoff game.

The only problem is that "lose to win" is a bad idea. Let me explain why.

In a baseball game, the *pitcher* decides what to throw at the batter. He may throw only junk at the batter, and most batters will swing at balls they shouldn't.

Sales is an entirely different situation. You should know what balls to ignore. If you are properly trained to identify qualified prospects and trained to relate, reason and resolve, you should be able to close more than three in ten sales.

The "lose to win" scenario needs to be changed into a "win to win" scenario. You should be going from one win to the next. Closing three out of ten sales is miserable, to say the least. By executing your presentations properly and winning more often with fewer losses, you will be much happier. If you are trained to believe that winning 30 percent of the time is okay when you are delivering a presentation to a qualified prospect, you will achieve that low expectation. However, if you focus on the fundamentals and pay attention to selling qualified prospects, you can achieve greater results and reduce the adversity of your job.

## *Playing the Right Card*

Having a well-prepared and -performed sales presentation is the same as playing the right card at the right time in a card game.

Once you have your sales steps in place, you can let them unfold as you play them just at the right time to win the sale. So, you should think of each sales presentation as a hand of cards, and the prospect is the other player. As the hand unfolds, you play various cards at specific times to get the desired effect—to win the hand.

During your sales presentation, you are making several mini-presentations to win multiple hands by relating, reasoning, and resolving to win the game (in this case, the sale). For instance, when you relate with the prospect and find out about them and they learn a bit about you, that is one hand. When you learn why the prospect is considering your product or service, that is another hand. When you explain who the company is, that is another hand, and so on.

If you think this way, you will become proficient at playing the right card at the right time. Playing the right card will help you have the right mindset, and this approach will make you an expert player in the game of sales.

# *Conviction*

All of us have certain personal beliefs or convictions about what we consider right and wrong as they relate to our own values and morals. Something that is objectionable to one person may be acceptable to another because of our differing values. In sales, conviction and enthusiasm are closely connected. If you wholeheartedly believe in your product, you are going to convey compelling enthusiasm. I can't even list the number of times I've been approached by or had conversations with a salesperson who didn't exude conviction in their product. It's as transparent as glass.

When a qualified prospect contacts you about your product or service, how certain are you that the individual would be better off using it? If you are not convinced that your prospects are going to have better outcomes using your product or service, then you need to reason with the most important person involved—yourself.

Do you believe in your company's product or service, and that what you are doing is helping your customers? Do you feel like you are putting one over on the prospect when you make a sale? Would *you* purchase the product or service that you are selling?

There are exceptions, of course. For example, if you sell industrial cranes you probably do not need to buy one. But let's say you are an insurance salesperson but do not own an insurance policy? Or you're a Volkswagen salesperson who drives a Ford because of your dislike of import cars. Or a vegetarian that sells steaks! I think you get the idea.

Be honest with yourself. If you do not believe in your company's product or service, then I have a recommendation: Find a company that has a product or service you can believe in, and go to work for them.

## *Focus*

In general, being distracted is a problem today. People are constantly looking at their smartphones when they should be concentrating on driving, paying attention to their children, or engaging in meaningful work tasks. You may face daily distractions like marketing, documenting and reporting activity, or the goings-on of operations. Also, what is happening in your personal life can be a distraction. However, when you are at the point of sale with a qualified prospect sitting across from you, you must focus all your attention on the prospect. Be in the moment!

The best performers in professional sports and other extremely skilled professions are highly focused. For example, if you are undergoing critical surgery, would you want your surgeon checking his stock portfolio during the procedure? Or, if you had a high-paid lawyer presenting your case in front of a jury, would you want him arguing with his wife on the phone during breaks?

A positive example of an individual with tremendous focus is Nick Saban, the head football coach of the Alabama Crimson Tide. Coach Saban does not let his players concentrate on winning the game. He has them concentrate on winning each play, one at a time. His team is trained not to think past the next play.

Another example is that of professional golfer Rory McIlroy. In a recent interview, McIlroy mentioned that even though tournaments are usually four rounds of eighteen holes per round, he only allows his mind to focus on playing three holes at a time.

One more example is that of Japanese competitive eater Takeru Kobayshi. At the Nathan's Coney Island Hot Dog Eating Contest, he does not keep count of the hot dogs as he is eating them. He is only focused on his process for eating each one.

As these examples illustrate, to be successful, we must be in the moment and stay focused when we are at the point of sale. Do not let your mind wander to other situations. Remain focused on relating, reasoning, and resolving with your prospects so that you get the result you want—the sale.

## *Stick to Your Knitting*

When the going gets tough, even the tough can wander all over the place and at times get lost. From time to time, the business environment you are working in may be challenging, and achieving results may become more difficult for many reasons.

What I have seen in many of these situations is abandonment from the course of action that has previously been successful. So, when adversity arises (and it will!), you must stick to your sales process and the proven strategy that works. It is always okay to improve upon it, but do not abandon it when things get tough. Staying the course may be easier said than done when things are not going the way they should or as fast as you would like, but fundamentals never change.

The basic tenets of *Relate, Reason, Resolve = Results* do not change. What we do within that framework can change at times, but we must stick to our knitting and continue relating, reasoning, and resolving. If you do that, you will eventually get the results you want.

The idea that adversity makes people change course is not new, and it is not exclusive to sales. For instance, when money managers are facing bad performance, they may stray from their established investment strategy to improve performance. So, when things got difficult, the manager deviates from his strategy or the fundamentals that made him successful in the first place. However, this very rarely helps, and it typically results in mad investors—they hired the manager based on the strategy that was outlined.

This concept also applies to pilots and flying. Pilots are trained to trust their instruments, stick to what they know, and not deviate from it in an adverse situation. When you see a plane crash that involves pilot error, the investigation typically reveals a deviation from training.

The point is that adversity can make us panic and start looking for an easier or more efficient way of doing something that has become difficult. So, the next time you begin to experience adversity or a decline in sales, work on the fundamentals. Relate, reason, and resolve. Do what works. Do not wander; the path will correct if you stay the course.

## *The Need for Practice*

In sports, we hear stories of individuals who are born athletes. In other words, they have the physical abilities to play a sport because of their height, their weight, how fast they can run, and so on. No doubt you have heard accounts of the seven-foot-tall young man from a country where they do not play basketball, or the six-foot, ten-inch, 350-pound seventeen-year-old whose only previous sport is playing video games. Now, is the seven-foot-tall young man going to be able to start for the university basketball team the first year he joins the team? No. How about the seventeen-year-old? Will he be the starter for the college football team his first year just because of his size? No.

If a company hires a smart, well-dressed, articulate, and organized individual, does that make him a salesperson? No.

Why would a company give a new salesperson some basic information about their product or service and a sales presentation and think they are ready to perform? They are not ready for the same reasons the two athletes are not ready; they need training and practice. They need an overall understanding of the sales process. A new salesperson needs practice, practice, and then some more practice.

I have been in sales for many years, and I practice every week. I am always practicing. I go over my sales presentation and mentally make sure that I am covering each of the key points in my sales process. Also, I practice sections of my presentation where I may have included an enhancement, or I have made changes due to competition. Additionally, there could be a new product or service that is coming out that needs to be included in the deliverables section of the presentation. Perhaps there could be a change in the delivery section of my product or service. For example, I may be running out of a certain product, and I may need to update my presentation and add urgency so that I can sell the remaining limited inventory. These variables are the reason I am always practicing my sales presentations and process.

Why do new salespeople not practice their presentations? It makes absolutely no sense to me whatsoever. You should hold regular training sessions with other members of your team. You can watch your colleagues during various parts of the sales process and critique each other. It should go without saying that practicing is an important way that you can improve your performance.

In addition to performing practice sessions, you need to analyze recent presentations, conduct post-mortems, or "watch film" on your past performances and think about how to improve. Sales practice sessions must be performed frequently and continually to achieve consistently better results.

## *Self-Discipline*

Successful salespeople are self-disciplined—they plan their work and work their plan. They make a set number of new sales calls every day and schedule a certain number of presentations a week. Success is related to discipline. Sales managers or business owners are never concerned about top salespeople working because they know that they are self-disciplined. Have you ever seen "We're looking for a self-starter" in a job posting? What do you think they mean by that? Simple: They want a disciplined person that can work a plan without someone hovering over their shoulder.

If you are struggling right now, it could be due to a lack of discipline. How does this pertain to R3R1? Once you come to understand the formula, you realize that you never master your sales process until you close 100 percent of all qualified prospects. You must never stop practicing to improve your sales process. If you do not review your process on a daily and weekly basis, you are simply on autopilot, and that is not disciplined. That would be like Tom Brady not running practice drills. He is not Tom Brady because he is undisciplined. If we watched his game preparation, it would most likely astound us. He would never go into a game saying to himself, "You know, I won twenty-five playoff games and five Super Bowls. I don't need to prepare or practice my process." Is that what you are doing? Have you stopped practicing your process?

If this is an issue, if you have never prepared or have stopped preparing, then get started now, and you will see your sales increase. Nothing happens by accident. Successful people are successful because opportunity meets up with preparation and experience. To be a top-performing sales professional, you must be self-disciplined in all aspects of your work, especially in your sales presentation process.

## *Perfection!*

Only twenty-three pitchers have tossed perfect games in over a hundred years of Major League Baseball history, but all pitchers *want* to pitch a perfect game. Actors want to deliver a perfect performance. The best salespeople want to close every sale. However, just like the perfect game and perfect performance, a perfect closing ratio is elusive.

The mystery of why someone did not buy your product or service may be baffling. The prospect was genuinely interested, could afford it, and met your demographics. You delivered a thorough presentation, but the prospect just did not buy. Chalk this up to the human factor. But despite this human factor, we must strive to reach the goal of 100 percent conversion.

Over a period of time—a day, several days, or even for a week—you may experience a streak of 100 percent conversions. If you do your best always to attain this goal, then you will put forth the effort to improve your craft.

Refinement comes by relating, reasoning, and resolving at the highest level. After considering all the concepts that I have put forth in this book, effort is involved in improving closing ratios.

You are not just going to experience some ongoing winning streak. However, just like great athletes who spend significant time training, *exercising* your sales skills will improve your performance and increase your closing rates.

# CONCLUSION

As you reflect on what you have read, what is the point? Have a compelling, all-encompassing sales presentation that is based on relating, reasoning, and resolving.

As I reflect on why I wanted to write this book, it is because of how much I value the science and the art of salesmanship. Being a salesperson is an honorable and needed profession. I believe that most people do not understand what we do and do not fully appreciate the importance of our role.

If you asked most kids today what they want to do with their lives, the last thing you might hear is "I want to be a salesperson." If you asked their parents the same question, you would be equally as unlikely to hear "I want my child to become a salesperson." It reminds me of the song "Mamas Don't Let Your Babies Grow Up to Be Cowboys"—just change the word cowboys to salesmen. It sounds reasonable: "Mamas, don't let your babies grow up to be salesmen. Make them be doctors and lawyers and such." However, in many cases, salespeople make more money and have more fulfilling lives than doctors and lawyers!

The good news is that every year, many people, young and not-so-young, are entering or re-entering the sales profession. Although they learn about their company's product and a presentation for their particular product or service, the nuances of sales may be harder to grasp. I am hopeful that this book provides the formula to help individuals just starting out in this business, as well as veterans in sales, experience improvements in their sales performance.

There are two schools of thought. One is to take some of the ideas and concepts from this book and use them to improve your selling. The other is to learn the techniques in the book, embrace these techniques as if you created them, and then improve them.

It is my most sincere wish that you find further success in sales after considering *R3R1: The Sales Formula for Success.*

# ABOUT THE AUTHOR

Russell M. Rush grew up on a watermelon farm in a rural community in Kansas. He left the farm at a young age and has worked in sales, marketing, and management for more than thirty years. He has developed a sales process into a software sales system for insurance agents and financial planners as well as a financial-based system that helps charitable organizations increase contributions and donor satisfaction. In R3R1, he shares a multifaceted approach to sales that works.

To learn more about the author and his latest developments, visit www.r3r1.com.

Made in the
USA
Middletown, DE

76136011R00116